GOOD VIBRATIONS

CLICHY BATIGNOLLES

GAUSA + RAVEAU
actarquitectura

AVENIER-CORNEJO
ARCHITECTS

GOOD VIBRATIONS
CLICHY BATIGNOLLES

TABLE OF CONTENTS

As the result of a successful collaboration between architects Gausa & Raveau and Avenier Cornejo, the E8 building located within Clichy-Batignolles's mixed development zone (ZAC) represents a pledge: a pledge that my predecessor, Bertrand Delanoë, had made to Parisians when he took office in 2001, and a pledge we fulfilled by giving the opportunity to this piece of "forgotten land" to reinvent itself.

It is above all a social pledge as the project harmoniously articulates a mixed program of 16,000 m² that includes both home ownership and controlled-rent housing units, a nursing home, a maternal child protection center and office space.

It is also an environmental pledge as, on top of producing energy, the 15-floor building features green roofs that contribute to its integration into the landscape of the Martin Luther King park.

And finally, it is also an architectural pledge as the structure, which rises to 50 meters, offers new perspectives for architects to build tomorrow's heritage, and for Parisians to invest in their own space.

Two years following its inauguration, the building has blended into the landscape as in the daily lives of those who live in it, work in it or pass in front of it every day, thus ingeniously combining the needs of a city that intends to embrace its modernity: population density, quality of life and compliance with environmental standards.

Embodying the revival of a neighborhood that has become an "eco-district", of a railway enclave that has grown into an urban ecosystem, it represents a vibrant model of sustainable development for the city of Paris, and it undoubtedly proves that Spanish and French know how to put things into perspective.

Anne Hidalgo
Mayor of Paris

The Clichy-Batignolles eco-district, which construction shall be completed in 2020, is one of the most ambitious urban projects currently being developed by the City of Paris. Architectural excellence, which is inherent to this purpose, should not overshadow the numerous programmatic, urban and environmental challenges that were identified at each of its design and construction stages.

Clichy-Batignolles's aim is to reinvent an urban enclave that is particularly constrained by the presence of rail and road infrastructure. Covering an area that is relatively small in relation to its program—more than 500,000 m^2 of the buildings are subject to a high programmatic diversity—the site has nonetheless enabled the creation of a major public park, the Martin Luther King park, which will cover 10 hectares in its final form. Hence the complexity of a project that aims to combine this large open space with a strong urban concentration. In addition, the project has some very ambitious environmental goals, particularly in terms of energy management as the district is aiming for carbon neutrality.

Designed by urban planner François Grether and landscaper Jacqueline Osty, the large central park is a key element. It is simultaneously a centerpiece for the green corridor in the north-west of Paris, a connecting space between formerly separated residential districts, a leisure destination for all and the landscape that can be seen from many of the eco-district's windows. One cannot miss its presence from the outlying streets, where it spreads through green spaces and can be reached through no less than 14 entrances.

The constructions take place not around, but rather at the outer edges of the park, without any physical disruption. Lot E8 particularly represents three structuring aspects of the Clichy-Batignolles project. The first aspect is precisely this intimate relationship with the park, which it borders on three sides. The second aspect is its strong programmatic diversity that includes different types of housing units, but also a nursing home, a maternal and child protection center as well as shops. The third aspect is its height: in application of a specific provision of the urban planning bylaw, Lot E8 is one of the 8 buildings of the project which rises up to 50 m, as well as the first to actually be built (the general scheme imposes a height limit of 30 m).

With its large area, Lot E8 was delimited so as to allow the construction of a couple of buildings, precisely in order to better manage these three issues thanks to a design led by two teams of architects. The result matches the expectations of the developer and those of the City of Paris. The park generously enters in the fault which crosses the very center of the block designed by Gausa & Raveau and Avenier Cornejo Architects. Medical-social facilities are at the same time open to the outside and out of sight. Green roof terraces complement the project's integration into the park's landscape.

As for the height, it is overshadowed by the dissymmetry and the horizontal swaying effects to achieve an impression of elegant lightness. Success is undeniable as the project, which was supposed to be a test, was carried out at a very sensitive spot in Paris.

Jean-François Danon
Managing Director, Paris Batignolles Aménagement,
a local public company

Covering nearly 54 hectares, the Clichy-Batignolles eco-district, including the operation we developed with our partner Linkcity, is a singular place that is located at the crossroads of several Parisian districts as well as in the heart of the central business district of La Défense and Plaine Saint-Denis.

As an urban reconversion of a whole new dimension, this district embodies the commitment of the Grand Paris (Greater Paris) in terms of sustainable development while being at the forefront of key urban issues such as the use of renewable energies as well as water and waste management. The district offers a unique interaction with nature in the heart of Paris. Here, the landscaping contributes to the urban biodiversity on nearly 10 hectares in connection with the Martin Luther King park.

As our group is strongly committed to the quality of life in the city and the creation of sustainable urban solutions, our participation in the urban revival of north-western Paris and the design of a model urban solution amounted to a great ambition. And it is with passion that we have devised a remarkable program, aiming for a genuine programmatic diversity that is consistent with the eco-district it belongs to.

Initiated in 2013, this project has accumulated 27 months of work. It combines Cogedim's expertise while offering its residents true architectural efforts to deliver quality of life. Consisting of two buildings, this complex, which has a total surface area of 16,000 m², is the first ever 50-meter-tall building of the Clichy-Batignolles operation.

Architects Gausa & Raveau and Avenier Cornejo have created a gradual elevation design that makes the most of the surrounding Martin Luther King park by offering unobstructed park views for most housing units. We have mobilized the Altarea Cogedim group's expertise to match the evolution of this district and to anticipate the needs of residents and users who nowadays work from the office spaces, as well as those of the child and maternal protection center (PMI), which we have also built. The contemporary architectural lines are designed to bring well-being and comfort to all residents.

Proud to have been part of this ambitious program that took place in a dynamic and strategic area of the capital, we operate responsibly in every territory. We stick by this societal commitment in all of our programs to deliver better quality of life in cities. This reflects our will to work for urban, social and programmatic diversity.

Laurence Beardsley
President, Cogedim Paris Métropole

THE CLICHY-BATIGNOLLES PROJECT

Covering 54 hectares in the 17th arrondissement of Paris, the Clichy-Batignolles project is by its size and ambitions one of the largest urban projects in Paris. Designed to connect and enhance the districts that surround it, Clichy-Batignolles is primarily a large, natural and crossing park located in the northwest of Paris, of which nearly 7 hectares (out of the projected 10) are as of now open to the public. This exceptional space is surrounded by an open and mixed district that combines all of the city's amenities (housing for all, offices, shops, facilities and public spaces), and will eventually welcome 7,500 inhabitants and 12,700 jobs.

As an ideal application lot for the City of Paris's ambitions in favor of sustainable urbanism, the environmental goals assigned to the district are particularly demanding. Energy saving and the use of renewable energies (geothermal energy supplying the heating and domestic hot water network as well as the electricity production using photovoltaic panels) help us advance towards a carbon-neutral district. Clichy-Batignolles is also at the forefront of the implementation of the biodiversity plan particularly thanks to the Martin Luther King park, which is part of the green corridor in the northwest of Paris.

From a housing perspective, the operation significantly contributes to the building of living accommodation as 3,400 housing units are delivered or under construction, of which at least 50% are social housing and 20% are affordable rental housing covering a variety of situations (student housing, dependent elderly persons, young workers, doctoral residency, etc.).

Strengthening the public transport service is one of the requirements for a balanced and sustainable development of this territory. At the completion of the operation, the extended metro line 14 and T3 tramway, which add up to the current service provided by the Transilien, the RER C and the metro line 13, will make Clichy-Batignolles one of the best connected districts of the city.

The ambitions for this district are also reflected in the iconic 160-meter-high tower designed by Renzo Piano for the Paris Courthouse, as well as in the architectural design of the programs that seek to make the most of the park and of the newly offered opportunities to build apartment buildings that rise up to 50 meters.

Launched in 2002, the completion of the Clichy-Batignolles operation is now well underway. On the park's banks, along Avenue de Clichy, 1,516 housing units, two school complexes, a day care center, a nursing home, a child and maternal protection center and 3,300 m² of shops and services were delivered. From now on, the buildings are being completed one after the other at a steady pace, which shall lead to the completion of the operation by 2020.

THE ECO-DISTRICT

Labeled "Nouveau Quartier Urbain" (New Urban District) by the Ile-de-France region, Clichy-Batignolles is one of the eco-districts through which the City of Paris has implemented an ambitious sustainable development policy, expressed in particular in its Climate Plan and Biodiversity Plan.

The City of Paris has recently adopted a Biodiversity Plan, in which Clichy-Batignolles is a prefiguration for development operations. In the Martin Luther King park, exceptionally rich fauna and flora are developing around a wet ditch and a biotope pond. The park is part of a green corridor which includes the Monceau park, Bois de Boulogne, several squares (including those of Batignolles and Épinettes) as well as the cemeteries of Montmartre and Clichy. This green corridor will be a major asset for maintaining Paris's biodiversity. In addition to the park itself, protection and development of biodiversity is promoted through the varied plantings along roadways, the landscaped and heart-shaped blocks as well as the green roofs. Environmental specifications impose biodiversity coefficients that are calculated from the project's revegetation of horizontal and vertical surfaces.

LOT E8

Covering more than 16,000 m² of floor space, Lot E8's program of the Clichy-Batignolles operation was awarded to the Altarea-Cogedim/Linkcity Ile-de-France consortium. Started in July 2013, the work lasted 27 months. Designed by the team of architects Gausa & Raveau and Avenier Cornejo, it consists of a mixed complex that includes the following:

- 62 rent-controlled housing units built by Linkcity Ile-de-France on behalf of ICF Novedis;
- 83 home ownership housing units built by

Altarea-Cogedim on behalf of the Caisse Autonome de Retraite des Chirurgiens Dentiste et des Sages-Femmes (Autonomous Pension Fund for Dentists and Midwives);
- A 40-bed nursing home and 6 day reception places provided by Linkcity Ile-de-France on behalf of RSF;
- A child and maternal protection consultation center built by Linkcity Ile-de-France on behalf of the Paris Department;
- Business offices built by Linkcity Ile-de-France on behalf of SDIC.

The architectural ambitions of the program are expressed by the construction of a mixed complex consisting of four buildings ranging from R+9 to R+14 on a common base. As part of the series of lots already built in the eastern sector of the mixed development zone, Lot E8 has the distinction of being the first delivered housing program of the mixed development zone to reach a height of 50 meters, thus rising to 15 floors. This operation aims to make the most of the Martin Luther King park and of the new opportunities to combine density and lifestyle. The distribution of the housing programs into two blocks of gradual height provides a broad perspective from the interior of the block as well as an unobstructed view of the park for almost every housing unit. Green roofs contribute to the integration of the project into the landscape of the Martin Luther King park and offer residents recreational areas. The complex is characterized by a strong presence of glass and white perforated metal mesh to clad the facades.

Lot E8 meets the particularly demanding environmental requirements of the Clichy-Batignolles operation and produces 44 MWh/year. It is H&E certified—Profile A Performance option and labeled BBC Effinergie.

BATIGNOLLES 08

The new Clichy-Batignolles district is part of the great open landscape of the green belt and is the link between the various districts of the 17th arrondissement. In this plan, Batignolles 08 is an emblematic lot at the junction of the main lines that shape this territory: north-south road, boulevard Berthier, railways, the Martin Luther King park. Unifying uses and social link, it has an extraordinary potential of centrality.

Batignolles 08 is a major multi-product operation carried out by Linkcity Ile-de-France and Nexity.
It is remarkable for its complexity which is expressed by the interweaving of numerous programs. Indeed, the project consists of 80 rent-controlled housing units, 153 social rental housing units, 72 housing units sold under home ownership, 42 housing units sold under social rental usufruct, but also an entertainment center, a movie theater featuring 7 halls as well as shops at the foot of the building.

Lot 08 is built around three 50-meter-high buildings including several housing programs with large terraces or balconies, a cultural and leisure hub consisting of a shopping complex, an entertainment center built for the City of Paris which features a concert hall and a movie theater.

The project's morphology was conceived so as to limit any obstructions on neighboring projects (Lots 06B, 07 and 09). Trévelo Viger-Kohler and Tolila & Gilliland, the architects in charge of this operation, also wanted an extension of the park inside the lot in order to ensure its perfect integration to the mixed development zone's environment.

Batignolles 08 is a complex project that is characterized by a strong interweaving of the programs, a high density, a mix of uses and typologies of housing and by the intervention of many actors that Linkcity Ile-de-France knew how to deal with.

ABOUT LINKCITY ILE-DE-FRANCE

For 30 years, the company has focused on developing innovative and differentiating real estate projects for all kinds of users as well as public or private investors. It is asserting itself as a major player in urban projects and land development.

As an urban actor involved in the construction of the Grand Paris metropolis, Linkcity Ile-de-France is developing new districts with its partners and its customers. For instance, it will start building the first zero carbon neighborhood called "Ilot Fertile" (Fertile block) in Paris, early 2019.

Linkcity Ile-de-France is also developing turnkey real estate activities, renovation projects or new constructions. As a matter a fact, it is currently building the Alto Tower in Paris La Défense.

Loïc Madeline
Chief Operating Officer, Link City

Oscillate, Vibrate, Resonate

Manuel Gausa

The L8 operation provides an answer to a rich and remarkable program of urban diversity, which consists in a complex of 160 housing units (accessible through home ownership and rent-controlled programs) divided into two built structures located on a large medical and social foundation, facing the new and vibrant Martin Luther King park, in the Clichy-Batignolles mixed development zone (ZAC).

As the architects responsible for the project's management, we were aware from the beginning that we were standing in front of a unique and exceptional site: a site that falls within the scheme of large parks and peripheral mixed development zones, located around the city of Paris, a site that indeed expresses a change of scale and urban music—or rhythm, if you wish—in this great nodal-place (just the opposite of what could be a *non-lieu*) which serves as a transfer space, both collective and connective, between meshes and tissues, between infrastructure and ecostructures, between built and green spaces, between empty and full, between urban impulses and citizen interactions. A big, diversified scenario of crossings and interlacing between scales, corridors and horizons, called upon to bring together domestic coziness and urban dynamism.

From the beginning, the purpose of the project was to work with movements in space more than with volumetrics. With subtle movements—rhythmic, resonant—more than with volumetrics that are excessively static or monolithic.

Movements that are likely to "move" and "vibrate" under different contextual rhythms and at the same time to nuance—or even to balance—the different heights that exist or are planned in the site. Back and forth movements, ebb and flow, which will endeavor to combine the idea of vertical thrust and that of horizontal vibration.

As if the city oscillated in this location.

The entire proposed operation could be described by these sliding and displacement movements, in footprints and height, involving four contiguous and/or pair-coupled structures, which rise separated by a large central "empty" space.

A strategy that would, on the one hand, respond effectively to templates provided in the Local Urbanism Plan (PLU) and in the specifications (adapting through successive withdrawals to the 45º standard line); one which, on the other hand, would prioritize the replacement of the closed or semi-closed block conception by that of the crossing block, thus highlighting the importance of this idea of breakthrough, directed from the park inward, which is likely to simultaneously unite, through frontal and diagonal connections:

- the park and interior fabrics,
- the front and rear spaces
- the front and rear blocks,
- the new volumes and the old corridors, through this central opening combined in turn with that of the other created side through the small belt.

Sliding effects and courtly movements which in terms of mass and through a delicately "polished" shrinkage highlight the presence of the Hotel Ibis and especially the vector force of Francis Soler's new building, with which the new complex strives to establish a somewhat complicit dialogue.

A dialogue, however, that is established with the other blocks such as those built by TOA or PÉRIPHÉRIQUES, by prioritizing a certain concept of rhythmic transition made of chords, alternations and replicas (in the sizes, the dimensions, in the openings, in the colors and the textures).

In these bodies that move between pre-existences, flirtations and connivances.

We do not seek angry confrontations, but rather friendly winks between different "urban factories".

Ultimately, our proposal seeks to focus on a coherent, and at the same time, differential approach in which diversity can be achieved not by addition or aggregation, but through variety and variation of a shared rationale: one that is capable of conjugating the idea of drive and corridor, the horizontal dimension (of the park) and the vertical force (of projections or overhangs), all from the sequenced evolution of these four pair-coupled structures which:

- respond to the same kind of shaping and geometry
- share a same-equipped stand
- rise with varying heights, separated by a large central void
- integrate and express on the façade, in a clean and distinctive way in each pair, an "elevated" housing program (with more jerky and vibrant rhythms, with shimmering and versatile reflections) or a «lower» housing program (with slower, quieter and more relaxed movements, with smoother and opaque surfaces).

On the one hand, this strategy makes it possible to respond effectively to the templates provided in the site, to substantially play with the context, to respond with precision and flexibility to the planned diversity and to favor a generous transversality (*"thorough, à travers"*), which in turn is able to ensure a good illumination and orientation as well as ventilation and sunshine optimized throughout the complex, thus promoting high environmental qualities.

We have argued more than once that "urban courtesy" should replace simple, iconic accumulation. The resonance, the synergy, the interaction between information, demands, situations and conditions (but also between formulations and urban formations, between signs and signals) should proclaim a new and more empathic and relational period where the "dignity of living—the great conquest of the 20th century—could today combine with the pleasure of living and living together.

This can be achieved through a more interactive architecture and urbanism, under a positive interaction mindset, both globally and locally, with the city (multiple) and with the context (unique), with the environment (sensitive), with the technology (*performative*), with society (of each generation) and with culture and creation (contemporary).

Manuel Gausa, PHD Architect, Chair in Urban Design and Planning, University of Genoa

ZOOM OUT
URBAN AND SOCIAL ENVIRONMENT

The Widest Vibrations

Ricardo Devesa

What should I observe about an architectural design? This question, which critics ask ourselves as we prepare to write about a building, also applies to photographers as they prepare to document a project. What should I photograph? Its façades, details, unique spaces — in other words, its architectural conditions, like 99% of building photographs? Very few photo essays and critical texts, however, set out to reveal a building's relationships to its surroundings, which tend to be less obvious. Ultimately, in this case, as critic and photographer, we both set out to describe an object and the relationships it establishes with its environs. One through words, the other through images. And where the work is done in tandem, both readings are mutually enriched. That was the case here. In October 2017, as the editor of this book, I joined Jordi Bernadó on his photo shoot, and he joined me in the writing of this text.

During a meeting with the architects, I proposed an approach to the building that is the subject of this monograph—located on LotE8, in Paris's 17th arrondissement, Clichy-Batignolle s—in terms of the "good vibrations" it generates on two scales of approximation: in close proximity and far away; in other words, between the two blocks rising above their shared base, and between the complex as a whole and its surroundings. In each case, our aim was to reveal the relational logics of the design. Along those lines, we divided the content of this book into two parts, called "zoom out" and "zoom in".

How close and how far away do these relationships extend? The echoes between the two blocks are explicit, through their dynamic play of volumes in recesses and overhangs, through the subtle references, parallelisms and contrasts between their material textures, and the iterative finishes of their respective envelopes: metallic, white, smooth and perforated in one block; and folded glass slats in the other. However, what is the scope of the relationships they establish with their surroundings? Which parts and elements did the architects hope would make their buildings "vibrate"? Over the course of our visit to the building and its surroundings, we both uncovered some of those relationships, which Jordi adeptly recorded in the following photographs, used as the basis for my analysis.

We stayed at the Hotel Inn Paris-Porte Clichy, located roughly 900 meters to the north of the building. The first picture Jordi took was from the window of his hotel room. In the foreground, we see a solitary Haussmannian building, facing Boulevard Victor Hugo. Behind it, we can make out the Boulevard Périphérique, the high-speed ring road that runs around Paris and its 20 arrondissements — built on top of the fortifications added by Haussmann to the capital in 1859. In the right corner, there is a partial view of the Tribunal de Grande Instance, a courthouse complex designed by Renzo Piano Building Workshop, conceived as a flagship for the ambitious new Clichy-Batignolles neighborhood project. It is now one of the tallest buildings in Paris (160 meters). In fact, the courthouse was conceived in the plan to be a new landmark for the city, on the same level as La Défense, the Arc de Triomphe, the Eiffel Tower and the Sacré-Coeur.

In the background of the photograph sit the construction cranes that are developing the site and, if we look closely, peeking above the construction is the very top of the terraced glass block that is the subject of this monograph. On an urban scale, the project represents the horizon for this new neighborhood, tying in with the even larger scale of the courthouse building.

The first day of our visit, we toured the entire 17th district. It was a Sunday. Martin Luther King park, an urban space that lies at the center of the plan, was chock full of people. The building on Lot E8 sits adjacent to the train tracks that lead toward the Gare Saint Lazare. The base shared by the two blocks has a small interior courtyard, which, together with the roof garden, becomes an extension of the park. Vegetation slips in between the buildings and, in turn, the buildings merge into the park. Few of the new designs in the area have proposed this kind of porosity and integration with the neighborhood's green lung.

The next day, Monday, we visited the western section of this ambitious urban planning intervention, still under construction then. We climbed to the roof of one of the finished buildings. Jordi photographed the opposite frontage, to the east, where the E8 building is located. The diptych of the panoramic view spans from the Sacré-Coeur in the south to the new courthouse in the north. From this angle, once again we see the strategy used by the architects to connect their building to the park. Similarly, we can read the contiguities between the white block (adjacent to the train tracks) and the one located two streets to the north (E10b, designed by TOA+AASB). In contrast, the transparencies and reflections in the glass block connect with the neighboring building to the south (E5, designed by Francis Soler). In this way, as the two blocks resonate with the surrounding buildings, generating an alternating rhythm, they are also perceived as autonomous with respect to one another, generating unexpected vibrations on an urban scale.

Architecture is constructed from the detail, to define its finishes, its material qualities. Generally, our analyses are based on a close-up perspective, the unions or articulations between the material parts and, from there, their spaces. And yet, the ethos of a design may lie more in its relationships with the surroundings on a larger scale, which may be hidden, or not as obvious. In building E8, the connections to the park, the cacophony with the adjacent buildings, and the subtle connections with Paris landmarks are all essential to creating "good vibrations" at every scale, transforming it into a place of places.

Ricardo Devesa, Architect, Editor in Chief, urbanNext

ibis
10

HOTEL

ibis

ZOOM IN

BETWEEN BLOCKS AND INDOORS

Good Vibes – Finding the Potential in the Constraints

Andrew Ayers

At a moment in history where cultural buildings—museums, concert halls, theatres, art galleries, etc.—seem to have achieved total formal freedom, taking on all sorts of bizarre and often gratuitous shapes, housing, especially apartment buildings, appears set on the opposite tack, becoming ever more standardized due to innovation-stifling predetermined constraints. First there are the diktats of the market, which encourage cost-cutting and conservatism in the interests of profit margins. Then there's the building code: the local urbanism plan (PLU), as it's known in France, which sets, among others, height and volume limits, as well as regulating the implantation of buildings on a site; but also the fire regulations, which introduce countless further limitations. After that comes global warming, which imposes considerable thermal-performance and energy-consumption constraints that hugely impact the architectural possibilities. And finally, in the case of a zone *d'aménagement concertée* (concerted-development zone or ZAC), there are the constraints imposed by the local authority with respect to programme and social diversity. Only once all these deciding factors have been established do the architects finally come on board, with the constraint of offering users the best conditions possible within the limitations imposed by this labyrinth of rules and regulations. The challenge, in such conditions, can seem nigh-on impossible.

It was just such a giant three-dimensional puzzle that confronted Franco-Spanish firm Gausa + Raveau and Franco-Chilean office Avenier-Cornejo (G + R / A-C) when they teamed up to design an apartment building at the new Batignolles neighbourhood in Paris's 17th arrondissement. Their allocated site borders the 10-hectare Martin Luther King Park, designed by landscape architect Jacqueline Osty, which constitutes the heart of a ZAC launched by the City of Paris in 2005—a transformation of former railway land that was master-planned by architect François Grether and for which the city set ambitious energy-consumption targets: < 50 kWh/m²/year for primary energy, and 15 kWh/m²/year for heating. G + R / A-C's project provides 145 dwellings ranging from studios to five-bedroom family homes, 83 of which, realized for property developer COGEDIM, are aimed at first-time buyers, while the remaining 62, realized by Linkcity for ICF

Habitat (the SNCF's housing subsidiary), are rent controlled. But the city further diversified the programme by adding to the mix medically-assisted accommodation for 40 handicapped occupants as well as a maternity centre.

For G + R / A-C, an urban amenity as exceptional as the park was something that should be enjoyed by the greatest possible number of occupants. Unlike the other teams in the architectural competition, all of whom closed the city block to a greater or lesser extent, G + R / A-C opted for total transparency between the park front and the rear of the lot by carving out a splendid void at the centre of the built volume. Wide enough to prevent apartments overlooking each other, the void ensures abundant air and daylight to all dwellings, allows a majority of them to enjoy a view of the park, and also permits the neighbouring building at the rear to overlook the park too. A one/two-storey podium contains the medically assisted accommodation and the maternity centre, with planted roofs that ensure the park's greenery continues all the way to the back of the lot. Both the COGEDIM and Linkcity apartments are divided between the two lateral wings, the sale flats on the park side and the rental dwellings at the rear.

If the building's lateral wings vary in height, it wasn't so much for picturesque effect but to satisfy the fire regulations: above the medically-assisted accommodation and the maternity centre, the number of floors is limited to avoid classification as an *immeuble de grande hauteur* (very tall building)—which would require permanent on-site firemen—as would be the case if the accommodation rose more than 28 metres above such facilities; but where the ground floor is free of specialized accommodation, the building can rise as it pleases up to the 50-metre maximum set by the PLU. There was also the conundrum of how, given the programme's density, the required floor area could be squeezed in, given that the majority of the available volume was taken up by a giant void. It was here that the architects had a minor stroke of genius: by widening the floors at mid-height via cantilevers of various depths, the necessary floor area was attained without calling into question the main design principles.

Furthermore, this extra thickness helps reduce heat loss, while a whole battery of solar panels on the roof (disguised as a standard floor) helps ensure that energy targets are met.

Through its different floor widths and varying heights, the ensemble vibrates to the rhythm of the constraints imposed by both the programme and the building code, which are further reflected in the façade treatment. On one side the building quivers to the rhythm of bright, white, perforated metal, while on the other its long balconies are cadenced by sparkling glass louvers. While it might seem that the windows' misalignment from floor to floor was an aesthetic choice, it is in fact a response to the fire regulations, which require a minimum vertical distance between fenestration; staggered in this way, the windows can be bigger. This is just one example of the generosity of spirit that prevails in every aspect of this building, and which is present in even the tiniest of details. Thanks to the architects' care and diligence, there's a benevolent energy that vibrates throughout and ensures that the most is made of the opportunities left open among the maze of constraints.

Andrew Ayers, Architectural Journalist and Historian

ibis HOTEL

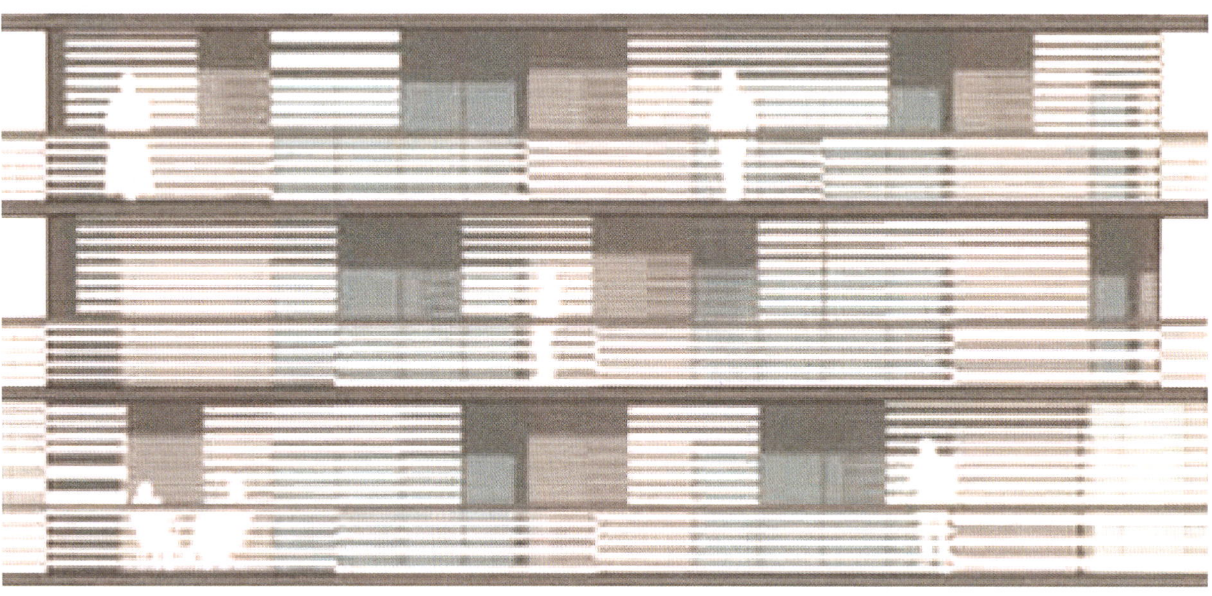

CONCEPT

THE COMPETITION, CONSTRUCTION, DETAILS.

The Competition

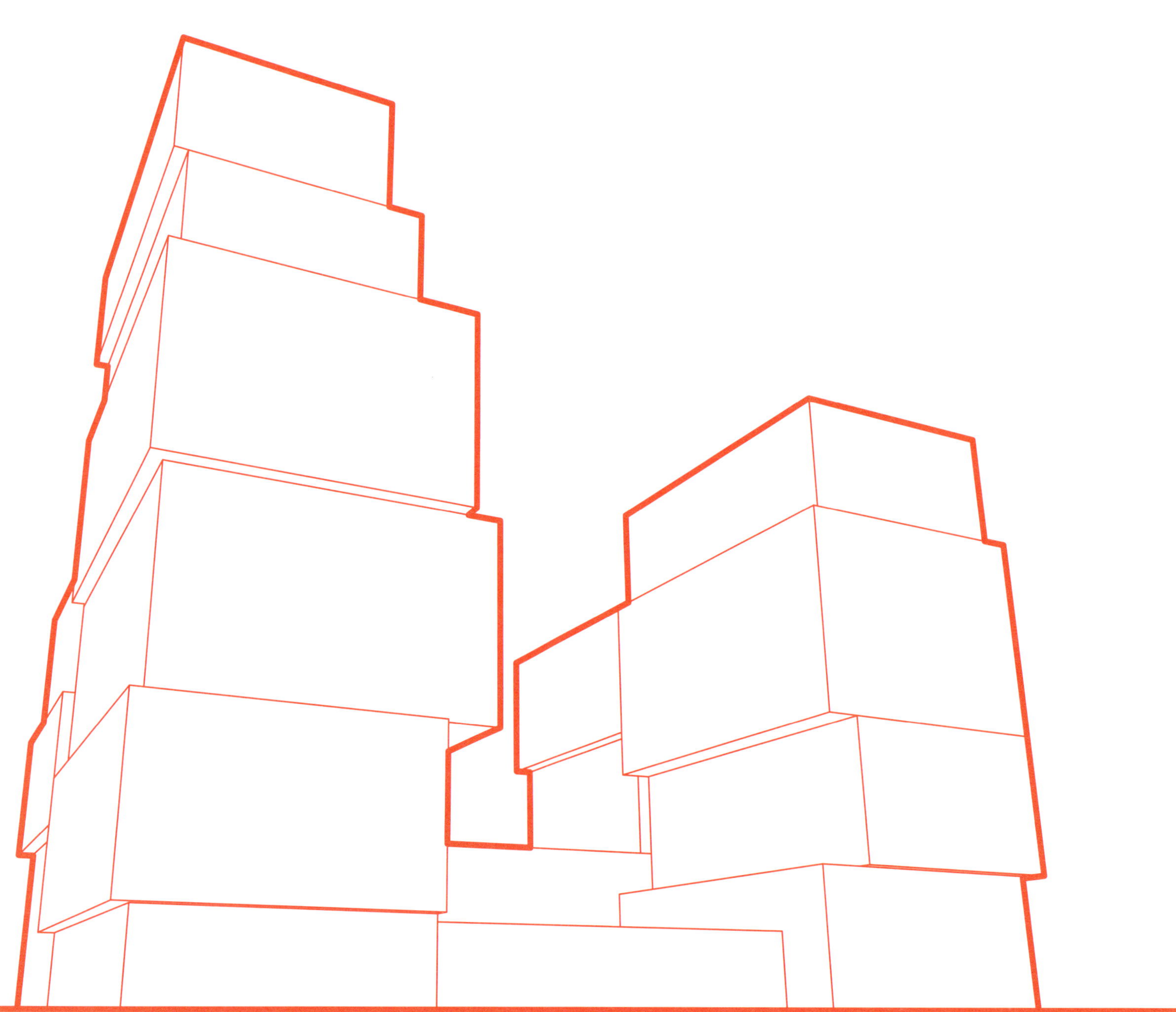

ZCB CLICHY BATTIGNOLES - LOT E8
PROJECT BRIEF

GAUSA + RAVEAU ACTARQUITECTURA
AVENIER- CORNEJO ARCHITECTS

URBAN INTEGRATION
LEAPS OF SCALE TO UNDERSTAND THE LOCATION

The site is embedded in the Paris interurban network, of the outer suburbs, and the principal green spaces and infrastructure networks. The Clichy-Batignolles Mixed Development Zone is seen as a fresh linking landscape, a major urban gateway opening up to the length of the major geographic spans towards the historic city centre.

The site becomes an important urban portal, an interchange hub within Paris's system of great relational spaces. It performs a role of transitioning between scales, whether the point of view is geographical, urban, environmental, social, cultural or infrastructural. Thus, the Mixed Development Zone works as a means of providing resonance and interurban transfer.

The Clichy-Batignolles Mixed Development Zone and Martin Luther King Park merge into a large relational space, an interface for urban links and relationships: lines of power and flow, lines of connection and interaction.

Resonating with the neighbouring buildings, the scheme seeks to prioritise urban dialogue, courtesy and elegance in a coherent and sensitive way, which prefers subtle movement to imposing gestures.

A TRANSVERSE BLOCK

One of the fundamental features of the scheme is the creation of an almost complete opening through the block, perpendicular to Martin Luther King Park. This opening works as a real extension of the park, bringing it into the heart of the block and taking it through to the street and beyond, all the way to Lot E9.

This way, nothing obstructs the view of the block from the park and vice versa. Thus, both the school complex and the housing enjoy relatively open views of the park. Moreover, a high level of transparency was sought for the plinth of the scheme, fulfilling the concept of maximising the linkage between the park and the street.

THE QUEST FOR COMPACT FORM AND FINE VIEWS

Well before the architectural design stage, this opening up also ensured that an environmental strategy was integral to the scheme. This provision involved the construction of much deeper buildings than would have been the case for a U-shaped layout.

Thus, the buildings created will be denser and more compact, considerably reducing energy loss. Moreover, thanks to this configuration, no dwelling will have just a single aspect to the street side. So, they will all have the benefit of overlooking the park and of optimum sunlight.

MASSES IN MOVEMENT

The two residential buildings are broken up into masses of varying heights; the highest building being 50 metres in height.

The blocks thus created are superimposed, then offset in relation to each other.

The goal is to create dynamic movement rather than static masses, rhythms rather than immobile hulks. These movements and rhythms, in association with the already rich architecture of the immediate environment, enable the invention of a new "music of the city".

This offsetting also enables the creation of more outdoor spaces and the optimisation of planning rules, particularly with regard to views.

The architectural strategy of this scheme results from careful consideration of how to avoid the building being classified as an IGH (high-rise building).

Paris, the Outer Suburbs

Integration of the site within the interurban system of green areas and infrastructure networks. The Clichy-Batignolles Mixed Development Zone is seen as a fresh linking landscape, a major urban gateway opening up the length of the major geographic axes and towards the historic city centre.

The City: a Leap in Scale

The Clichy-Batignolles Mixed Development Zone as a major urban platform, an interchange hub integrated into the system of Paris's major relational spaces and, at the same time, with a new multi-scale interchange role operating at various levels (geographic, urban, environmental, social, cultural, infrastructural etc.).The Mixed Development Zone seen as a means of providing resonance and interurban transfer.

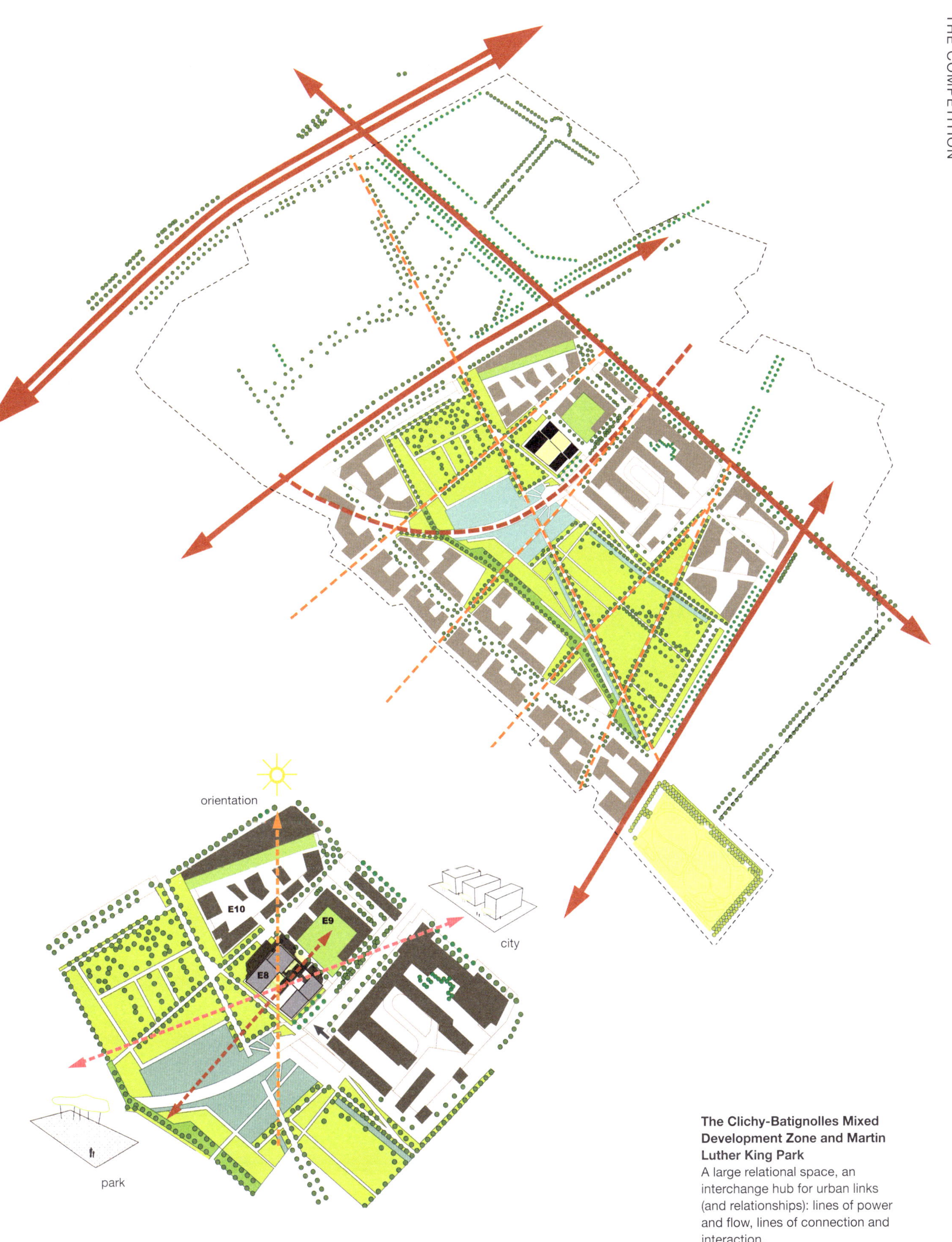

The Clichy-Batignolles Mixed Development Zone and Martin Luther King Park
A large relational space, an interchange hub for urban links (and relationships): lines of power and flow, lines of connection and interaction.

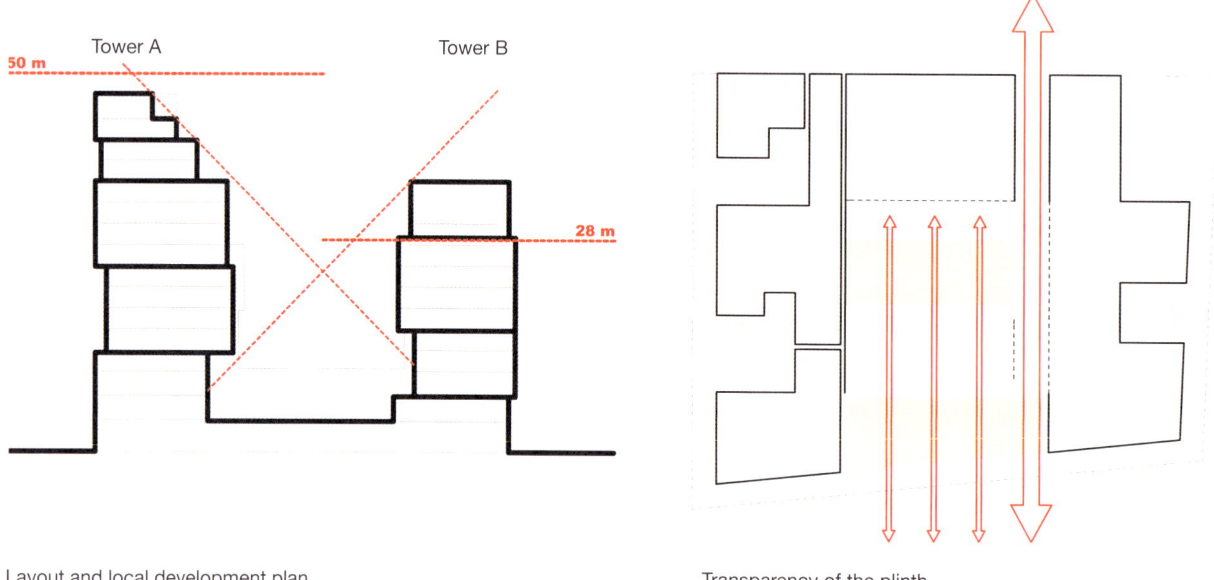

Layout and local development plan

Transparency of the plinth

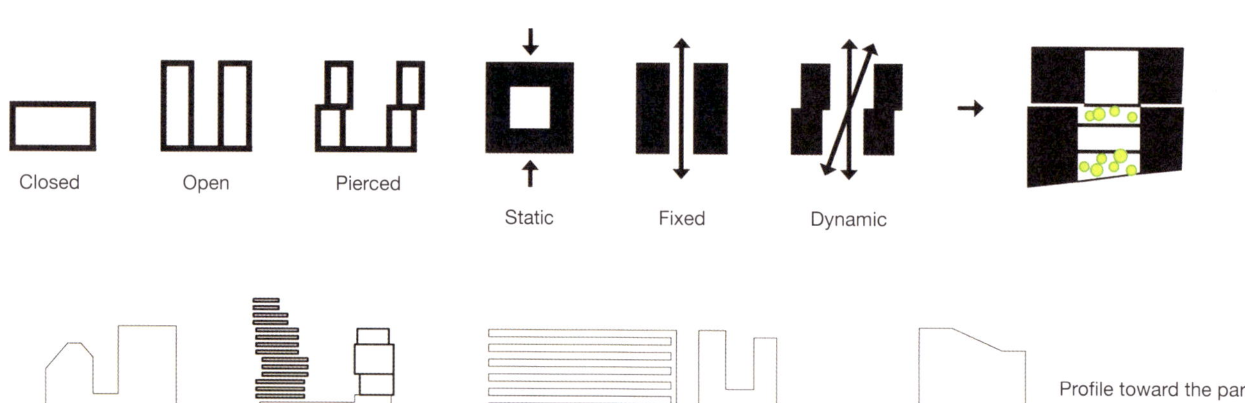

Town planning rhythm and movement

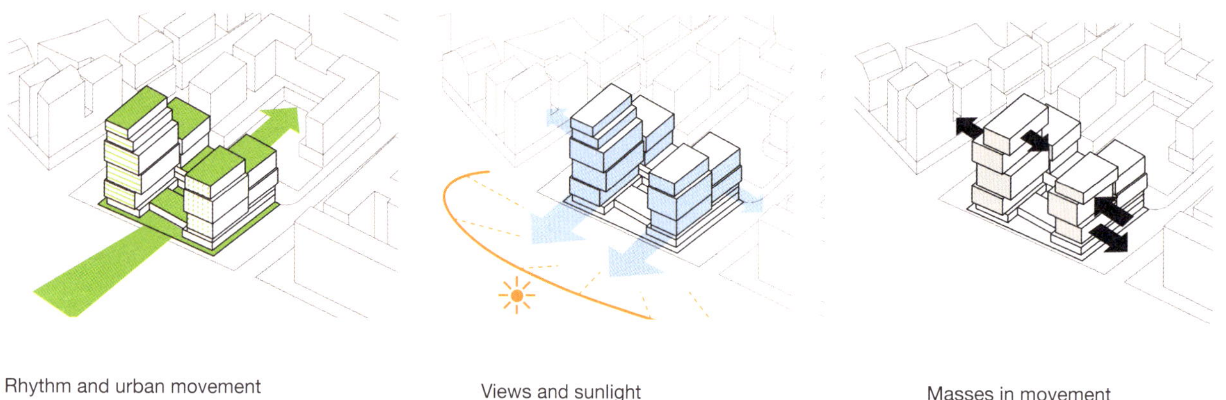

Rhythm and urban movement

Views and sunlight

Masses in movement

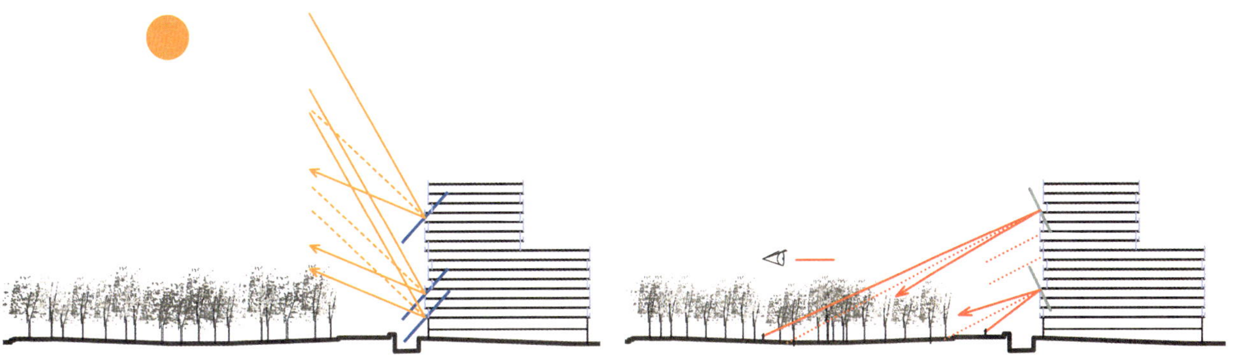

Eco-efficiency cross-section and facade drawing (solar filter and reflection of park)

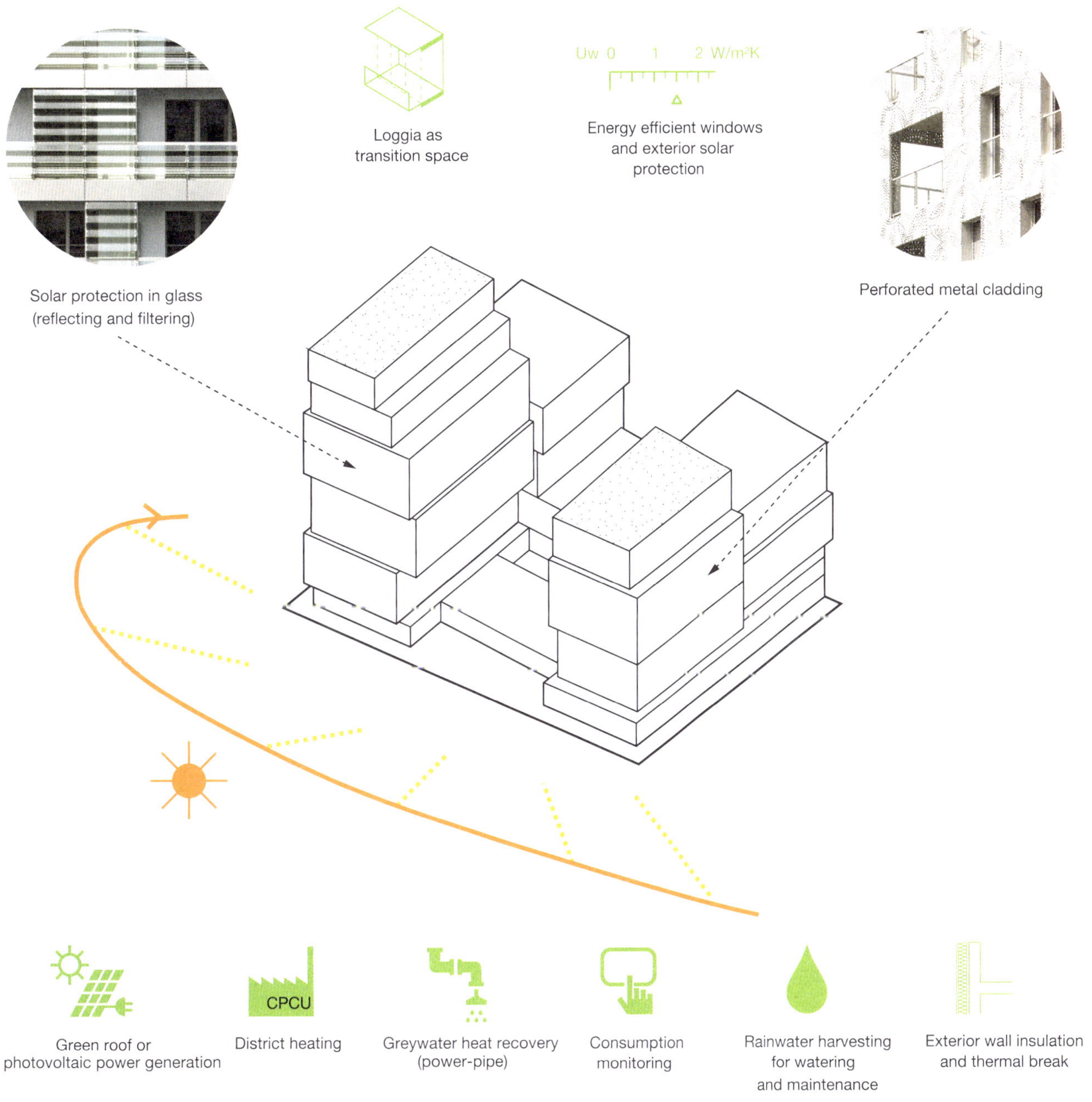

Loggia as transition space

Uw 0 1 2 W/m^{2}K

Energy efficient windows and exterior solar protection

Solar protection in glass (reflecting and filtering)

Perforated metal cladding

Green roof or photovoltaic power generation

CPCU

District heating

Greywater heat recovery (power-pipe)

Consumption monitoring

Rainwater harvesting for watering and maintenance

Exterior wall insulation and thermal break

The right level of environmental efficiency

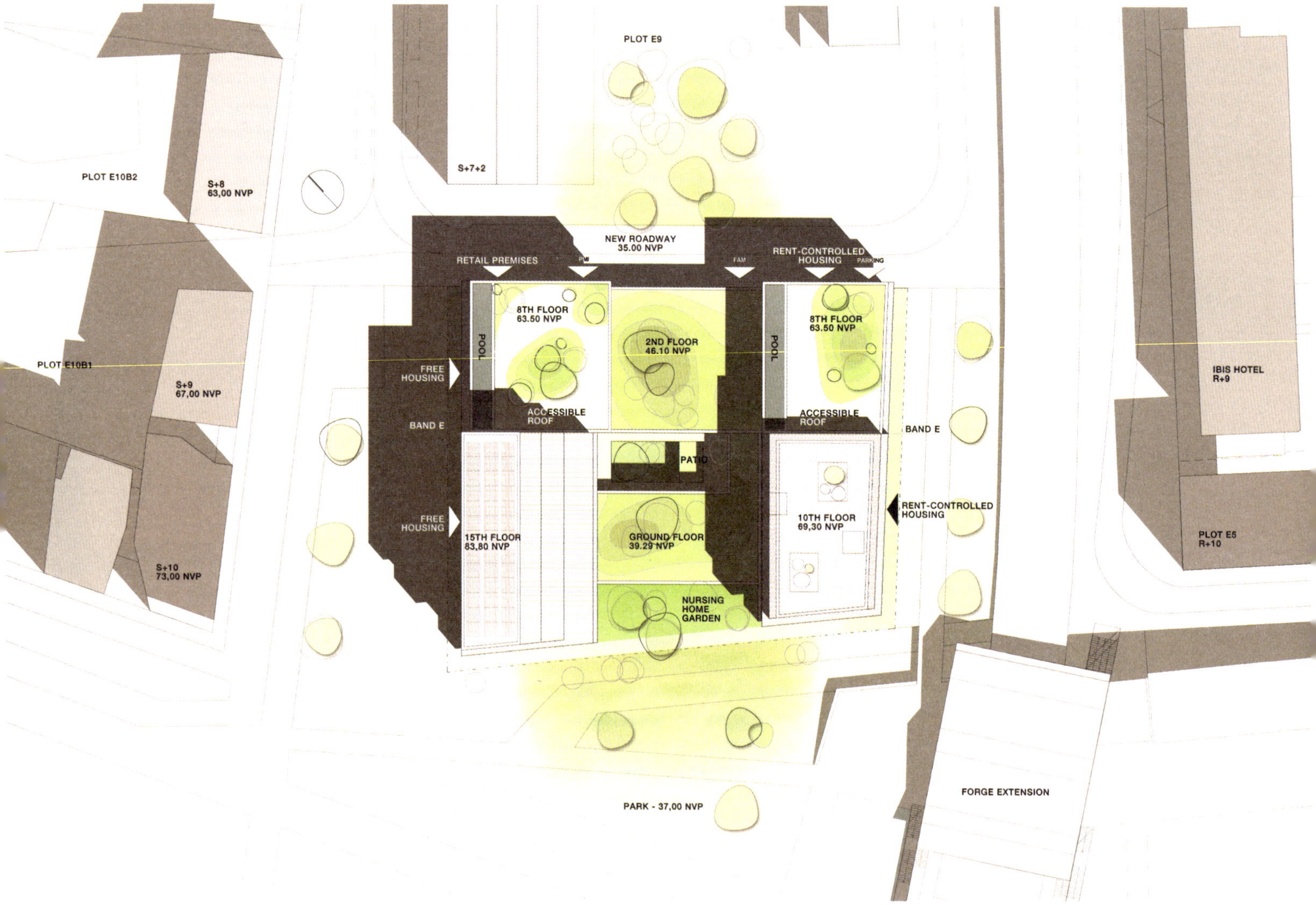

PLOT E9
PLOT E10B2
S+8
63,00 NVP
S+7+2
NEW ROADWAY
35.00 NVP
RETAIL PREMISES
RENT-CONTROLLED
HOUSING
PLOT E10B1
8TH FLOOR
63.50 NVP
2ND FLOOR
46.10 NVP
8TH FLOOR
63.50 NVP
POOL
POOL
FREE
HOUSING
S+9
67,00 NVP
ACCESSIBLE
ROOF
ACCESSIBLE
ROOF
IBIS HOTEL
R+9
BAND E
BAND E
PATIO
FREE
HOUSING
RENT-CONTROLLED
HOUSING
15TH FLOOR
83,80 NVP
GROUND FLOOR
39.29 NVP
10TH FLOOR
69,30 NVP
PLOT E5
R+10
S+10
73,00 NVP
NURSING
HOME
GARDEN
FORGE EXTENSION
PARK - 37,00 NVP

Location plan

BOULEVARD BERTHIER
PROMONTOIR
BERTHIER
PLOT E10.B
TOA
A PATH IN THE PARK
COMPETITION FEASIBILITY STUDIES:
PLOTS E8 AND E9
EXTENSION OF THE FORGE
(SCHEME FOR COMPETITION

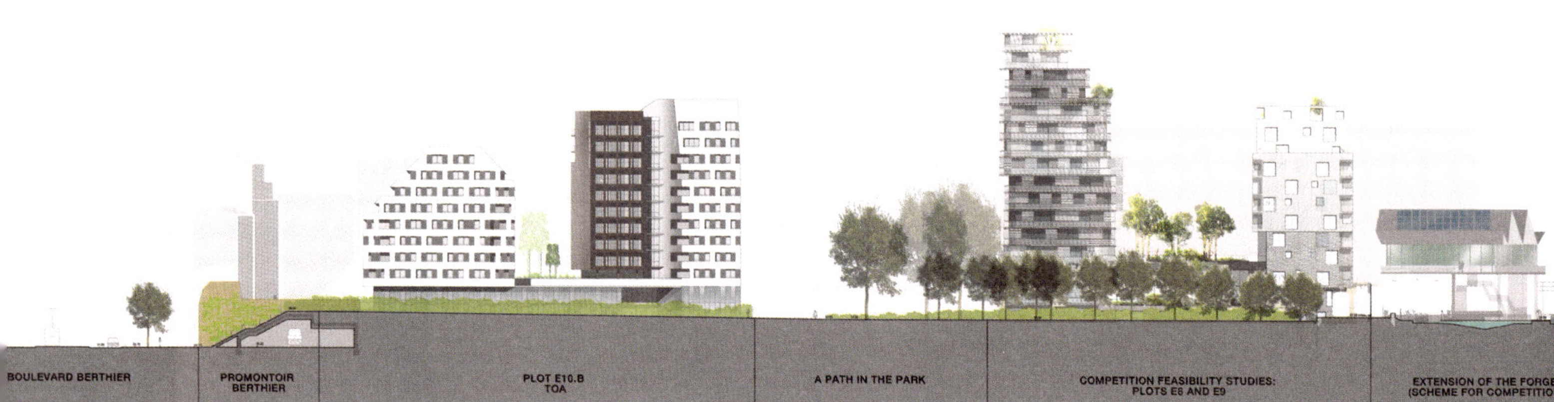

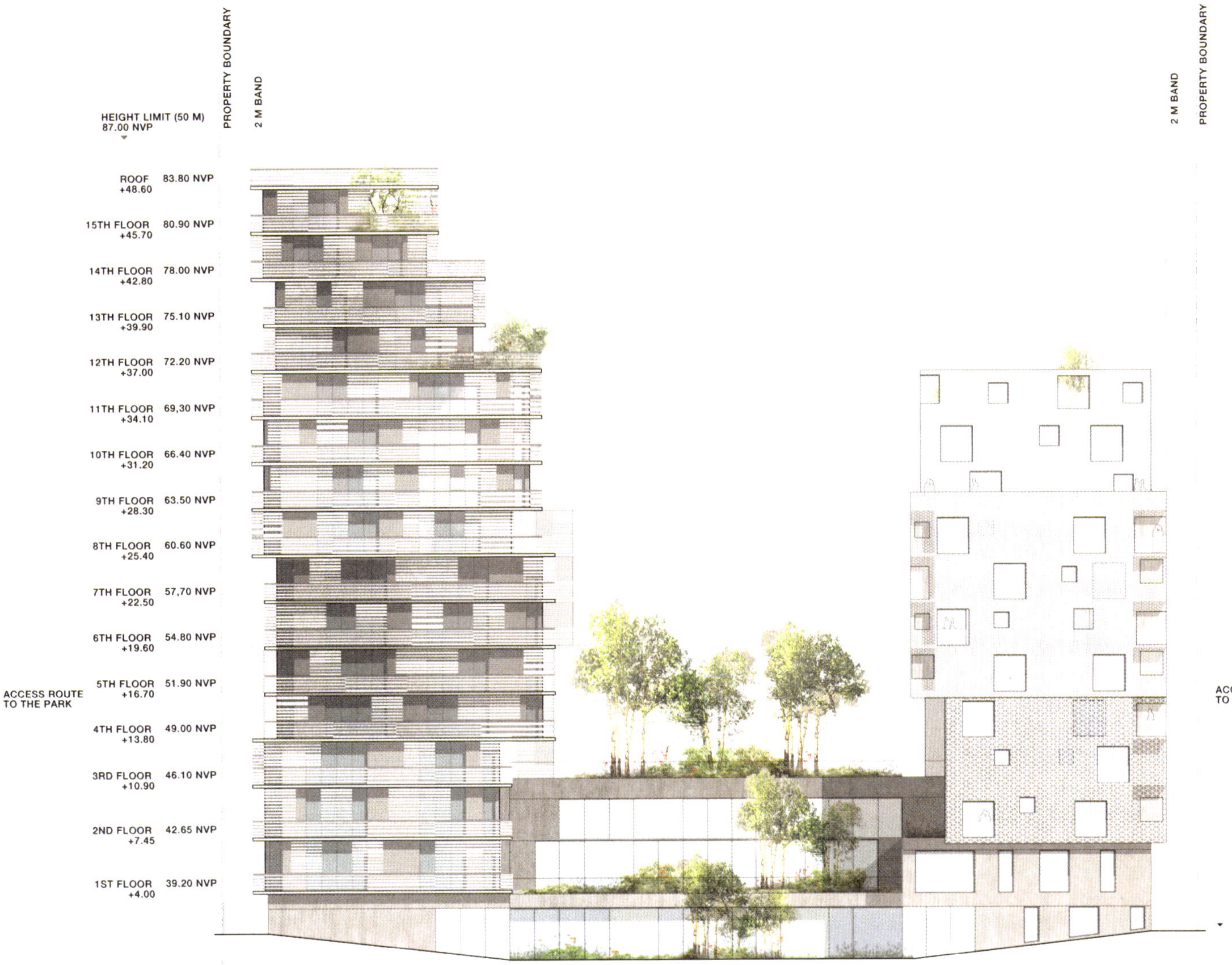

PROPERTY BOUNDARY
2 M BAND
HEIGHT LIMIT (50 M)
87.00 NVP
ROOF 83.80 NVP +48.60
15TH FLOOR 80.90 NVP +45.70
14TH FLOOR 78.00 NVP +42.80
13TH FLOOR 75.10 NVP +39.90
12TH FLOOR 72.20 NVP +37.00
11TH FLOOR 69,30 NVP +34.10
10TH FLOOR 66.40 NVP +31.20
9TH FLOOR 63.50 NVP +28.30
8TH FLOOR 60.60 NVP +25.40
7TH FLOOR 57,70 NVP +22.50
6TH FLOOR 54.80 NVP +19.60
5TH FLOOR 51.90 NVP +16.70
4TH FLOOR 49.00 NVP +13.80
3RD FLOOR 46.10 NVP +10.90
2ND FLOOR 42.65 NVP +7.45
1ST FLOOR 39.20 NVP +4.00
ACCESS ROUTE TO THE PARK
2 M BAND
PROPERTY BOUNDARY
ACCESS ROUTE TO THE PARK

Park south-west elevation

THE FORGE
PLOT E5 FRANCIS SOLER
PLOT E5 PHILEAS
PLOT E6 BP ARCHITECTES ATELIER DU PONT
PLOT E2 RING ROADT
PLOT E1 FRANKLIN AZZ

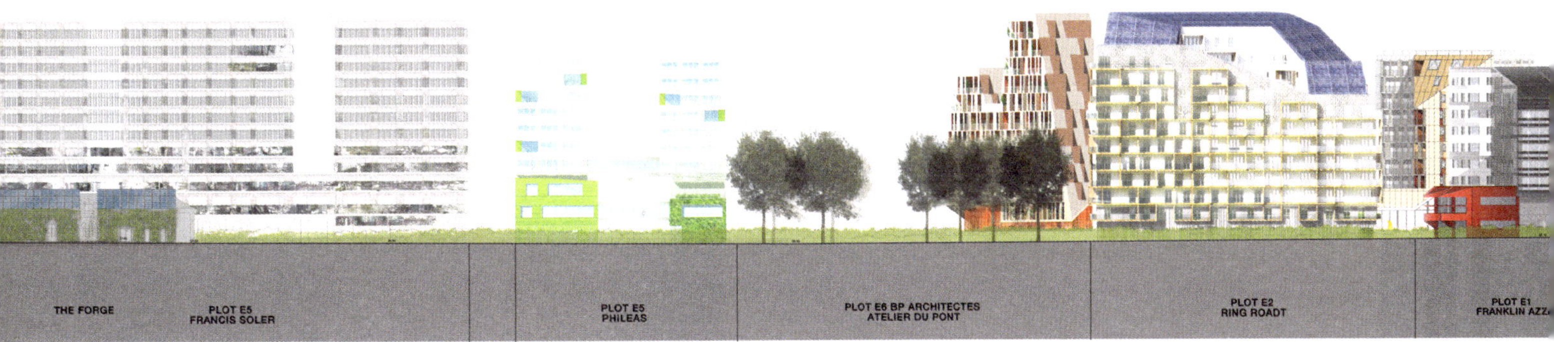

Skyline

Framing a fine romantic landscape.
Antoine Duclaux, Queen Hortense at Aix-les-Bains, 1813

Detailed view of the B building facade

Detailed view of the B building facade

Preliminary axonometric view of the B building facades

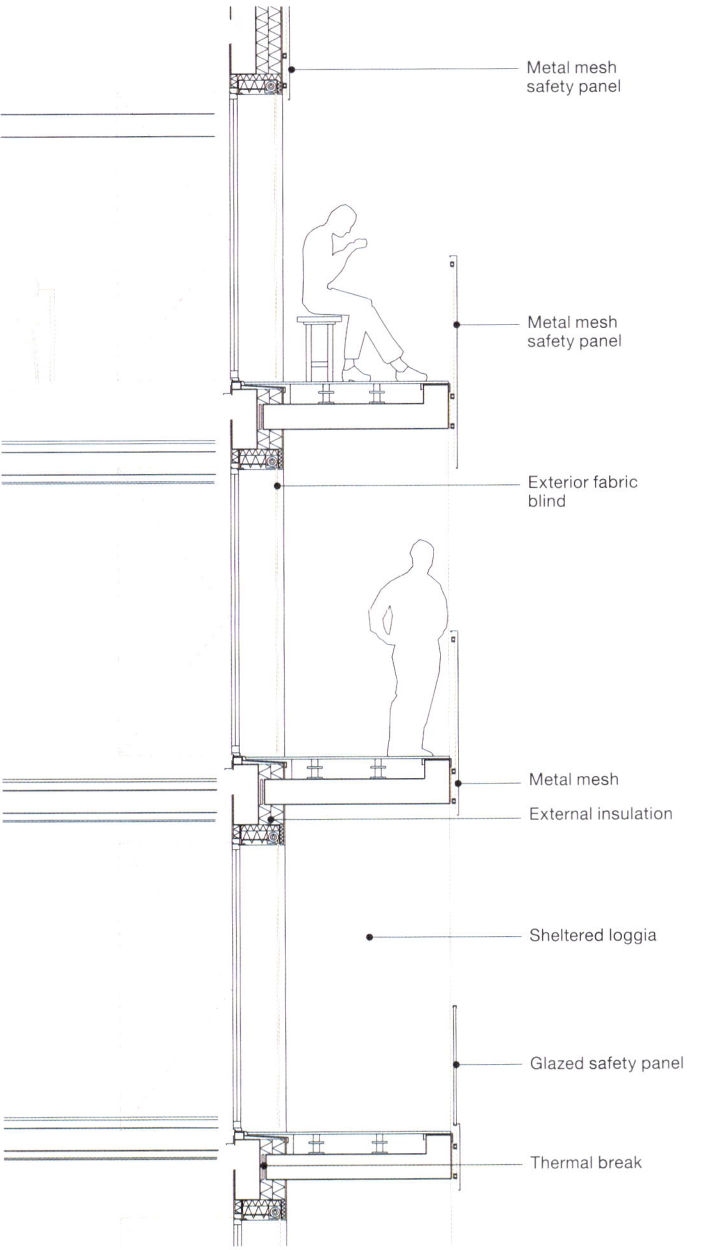

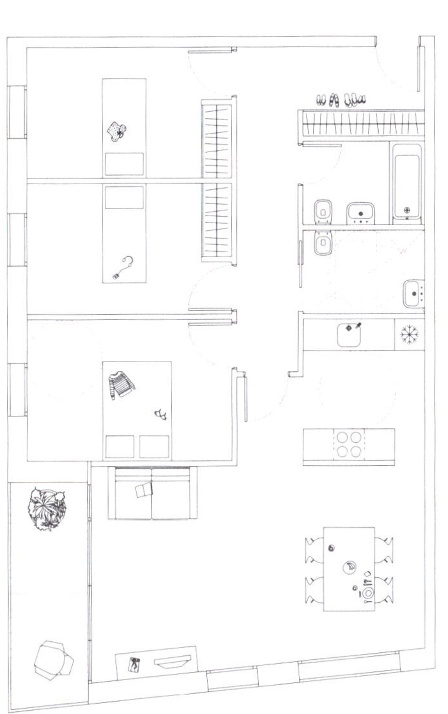

B building: Implementation details of home-ownership scheme housing, standard plan (86.5 m²) studio apartment.

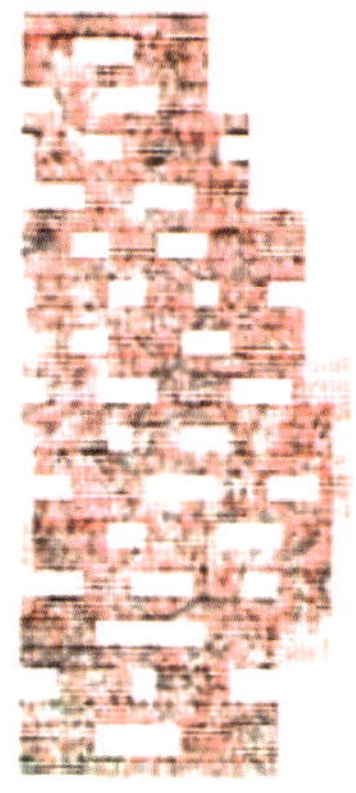

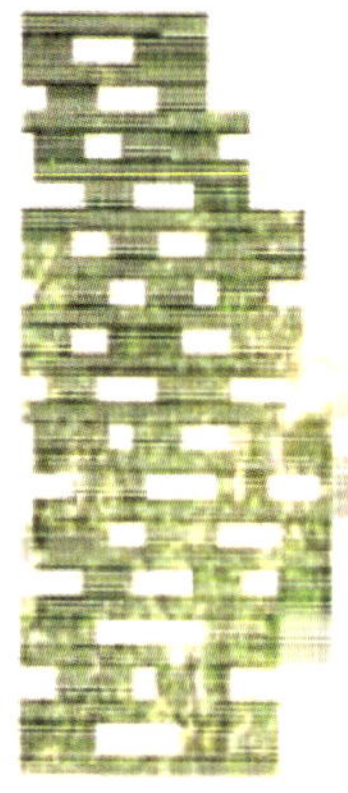

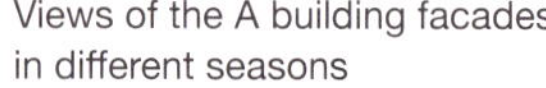

Views of the A building facades
in different seasons

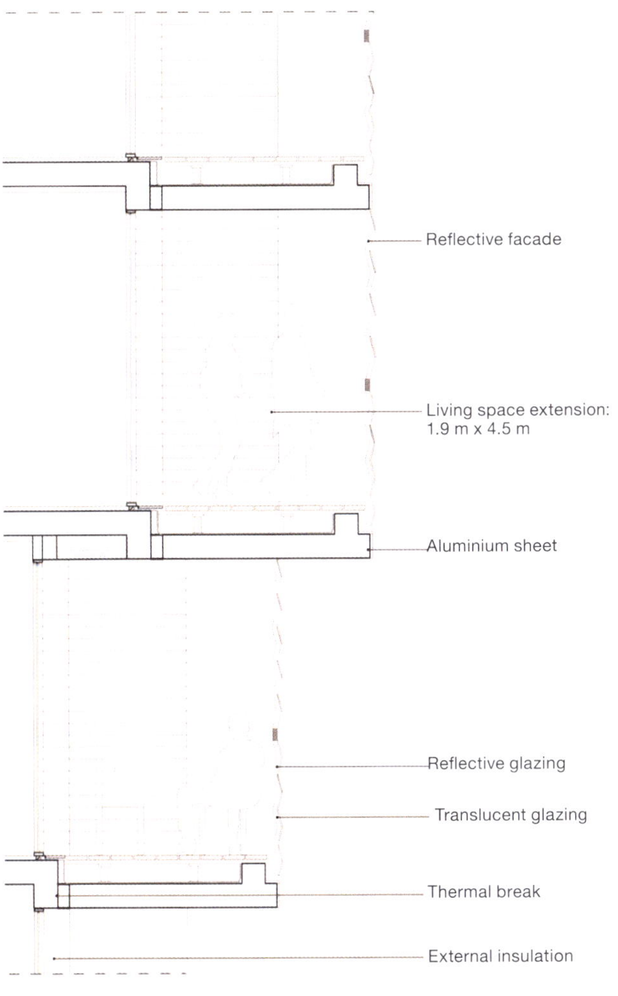

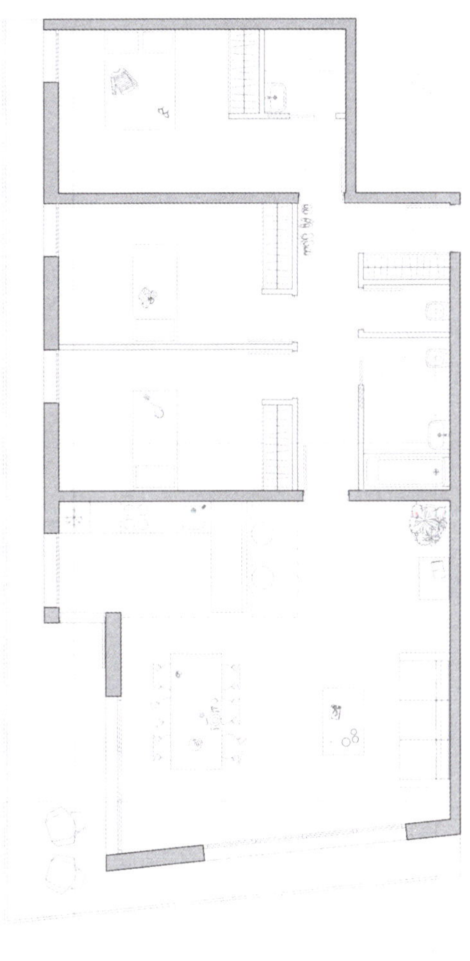

A building: Implementation details of 3-bed home-ownership scheme dwellings and plant (106.4 m²).

South-west elevation

North-west elevation

North-east elevation

South-east elevation

AA cross-section

BB cross-section

TECHNICAL DETAILS

Project Name:
ZAC Clichy Batignolles Lot E8, Paris 17
145 housing units + FAM + PMI

Associated Architects:
GAUSA+RAVEAU actarquitectura SLP and
AVENIER CORNEJO architectes

Project Managers:
Florence RAVEAU, Manuel GAUSA,
Mickael DOMINGUEZ, Vicky LENZ,
Christelle AVENIER, Miguel CORNEJO,
Olivier SARAMITO, Joachim BAKARY.

Project Team:
CFERM Ingénierie (MEP()
Bureau Michel FORGUE (cost estimating)
Franck Boutté Consultants (environmental engineer - HQE)
Bassinet Turquin (landscape architect)

Client:
LINKCITY ÎLE-DE-FRANCE and ALTAREA COGEDIM

Urban Planner:
Paris Batignolles Aménagement

Program:
145 housing units (83 housing units + 62 rent stabilized apartment units),
Disability care center (FAM: Foyer d'Aide Médicalisé) 40 beds,
Mother and child protection center (PMI: Protection Maternelle et Infantile),
parking (144 spaces).

Location:
Paris 75017, France - 38, 40-42,
50-52 rue Gilbert Cesbron, Paris 17ème
FAM: 48 rue Gilbert Cesbron, PMI: 46 rue Gilbert Cesbron

Environmental Performance HQE
(High Environmental Quality):
• Certification Habitat & Environnement profil A
• Certification BBC effinergie
• Thermal performance of buildings with reduced heating requirements at 14 kwh/m^2 / year
• Respect of the Climate Plan of the City of Paris
• Photovoltaic production required: 44 MWh€ / year

Date of competition: 2011
Date of request: 2011
Date of construction: 2013-2016

Site surface:
3,215 m^2

Built surface:
16,025.30 m^2

Used floor area:
Housing: 10,465.40 m^2 (excl. garden)
FAM: 3,078.60 m^2 PMI: 253 m^2

Budget:
33,792,621.00 € HT

Consultants:
Les produits de l'épicerie (graphic design)
EVP Ingénierie (structural engineer)

Construction Company:
Bouygues Bâtiment Île-de-France

The CPEDD audit of the project was evaluated on the following criteria:

• Consomption objectives (the following objectives were negotiated in the PRO-DCE phase):
- Heating: set to 17.3 kWhep/m^2/year initially, we reached 11.6 kWhep/m^2/year.
- ECS: set to 23.1 kWhep/m^2/year year initially, we reached 22.6 kWhep/m^2/year.
- Collective Electricity Consumption: 43.2 kWhep/m^2/year initially, we reached 42.9 kWhep/m^2/year.

• The Plan Climate: conformity achieved - total consumption level bellows 50 kWh/m^2 SHON / year - (48 kWh/m^2/year).

• Photovoltaic production: 49,790 kWhef/year (i.e., 49.8 MWhef/year)

• Permeability & FAM/PMI: the test must be inferior to 1 m3/h.m^2. Two tests A and B were successful (A: 0.309 and B: 0.49 m^3/m^2 h). Test for FAM/PMI yet to be scheduled.

• The thermo-dynamic simulations detected the necessity to ventilate some units in the summer (i.e., opening windows) and the installation of sun protection equipment.

GOOD VIBRATIONS - CLICHY BATIGNOLLES

HALL
FAM

The Executive Plan

South-west elevation

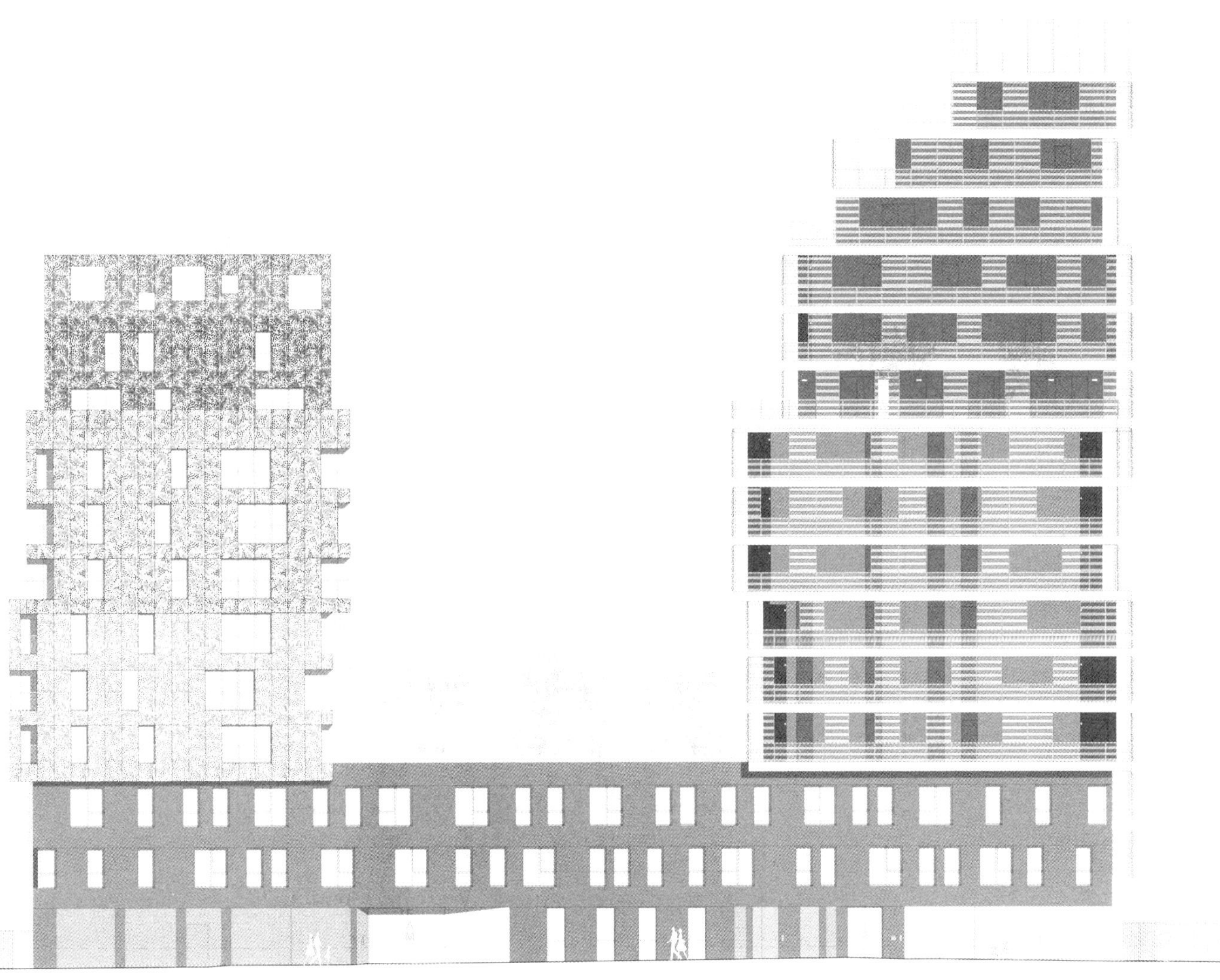

North-east elevation

South-east elevation

North-west elevation

West facade cross-section

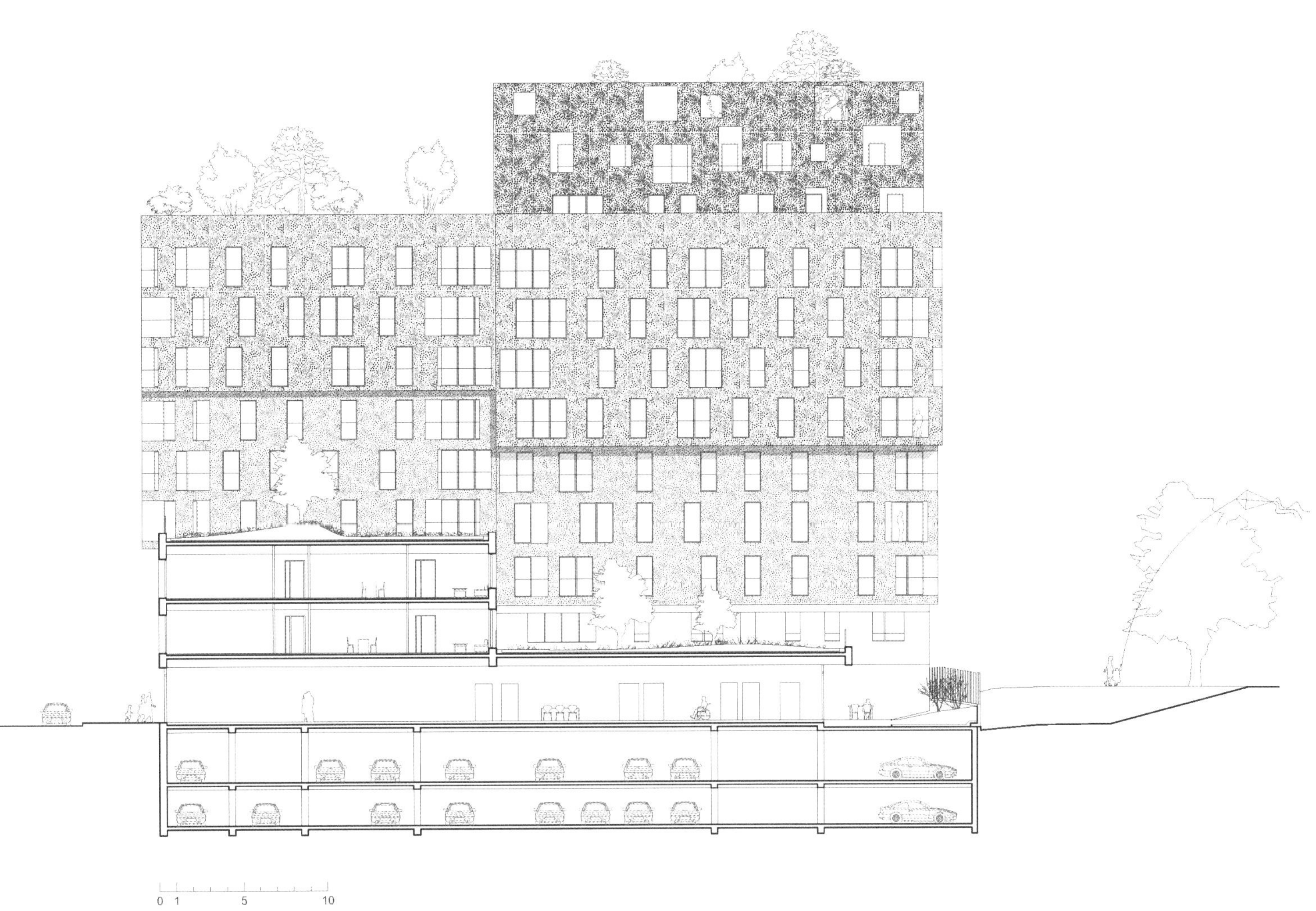

East facade cross-section

Ground floor plan

01 Reception
02 Waiting/activity
03 Doctors surgery
04 Weighing and measuring
05 Entrance hall
06 Dustbins
07 Bicycles/pushchairs
08 Entrance hall A1
09 Staff room
10 Laundry room
11 Sanitary facilities
12 Storage
13 Common room / dining room
14 Sluice
15 Retail premises
16 Management
17 Multipurpose room
18 Activity room
19 Office
20 Kitchen
21 Patio
22 Doctors surgery / treatment room
23 Family area
24 Common room / dining room
25 Psychologist
26 Multisensory (Snoezelen) room
27 Beauty salon
28 Occupational therapy
29 Psychomotility
30 Physiotherapy
31 Transformer
32 Caretaker's lodge

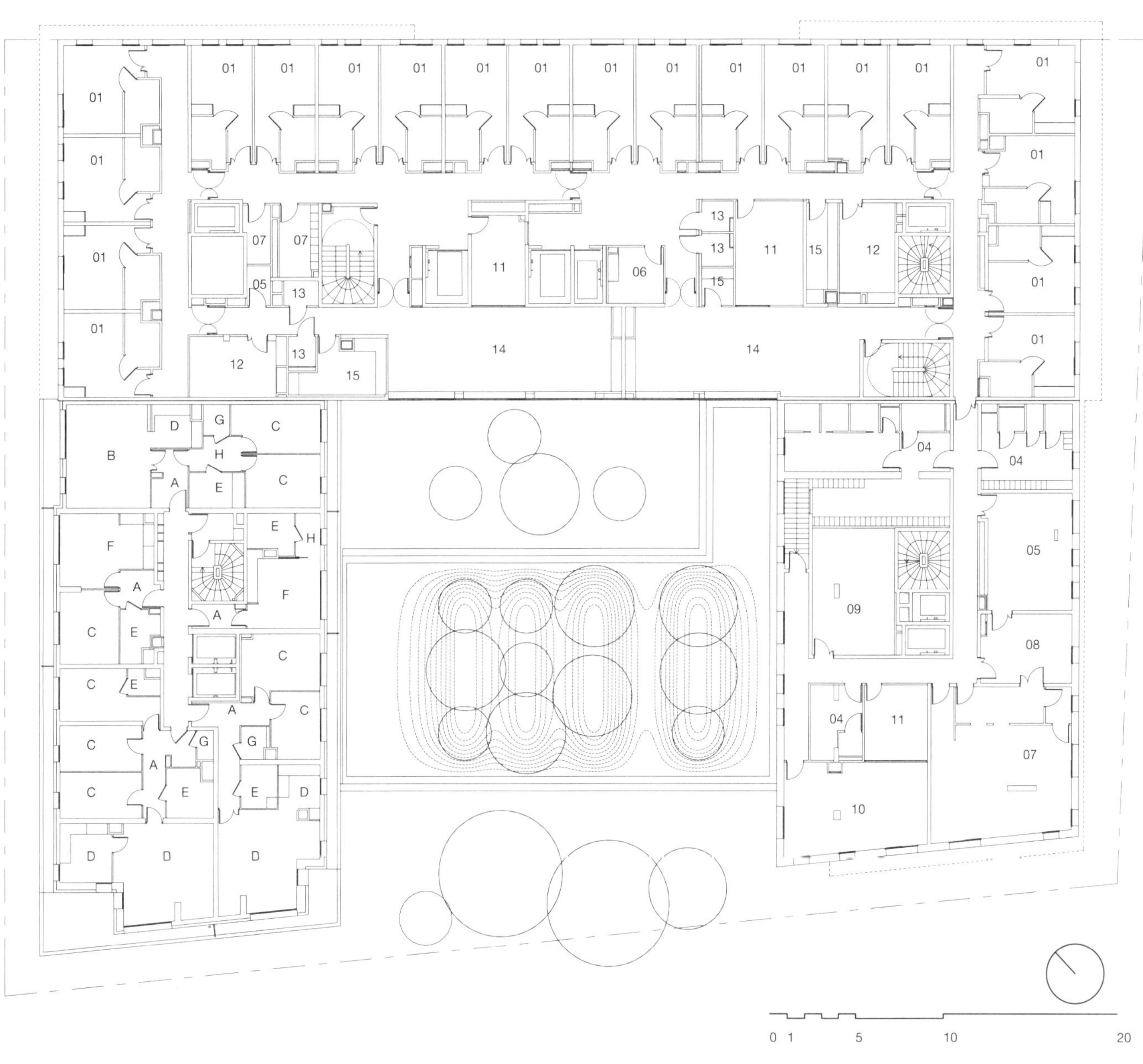

First floor

Nursing home
01 Bedroom type A
02 Bedroom type B
03 Bedroom type C
04 Cloakroom
05 Equipment maintenance
06 Treatment room
07 Laundry room
08 Store room
09 Archives
10 Rest area – Staff dining room
11 Office
12 Bathroom
13 Sanitary facilities
14 Lounge
15 Storage

Housing
A Entrance hall
B Living room
C Bedroom
D Kitchen
E Bathroom
F Living room / kitchen
G WC
H Circulation areas
I Terrace/loggia

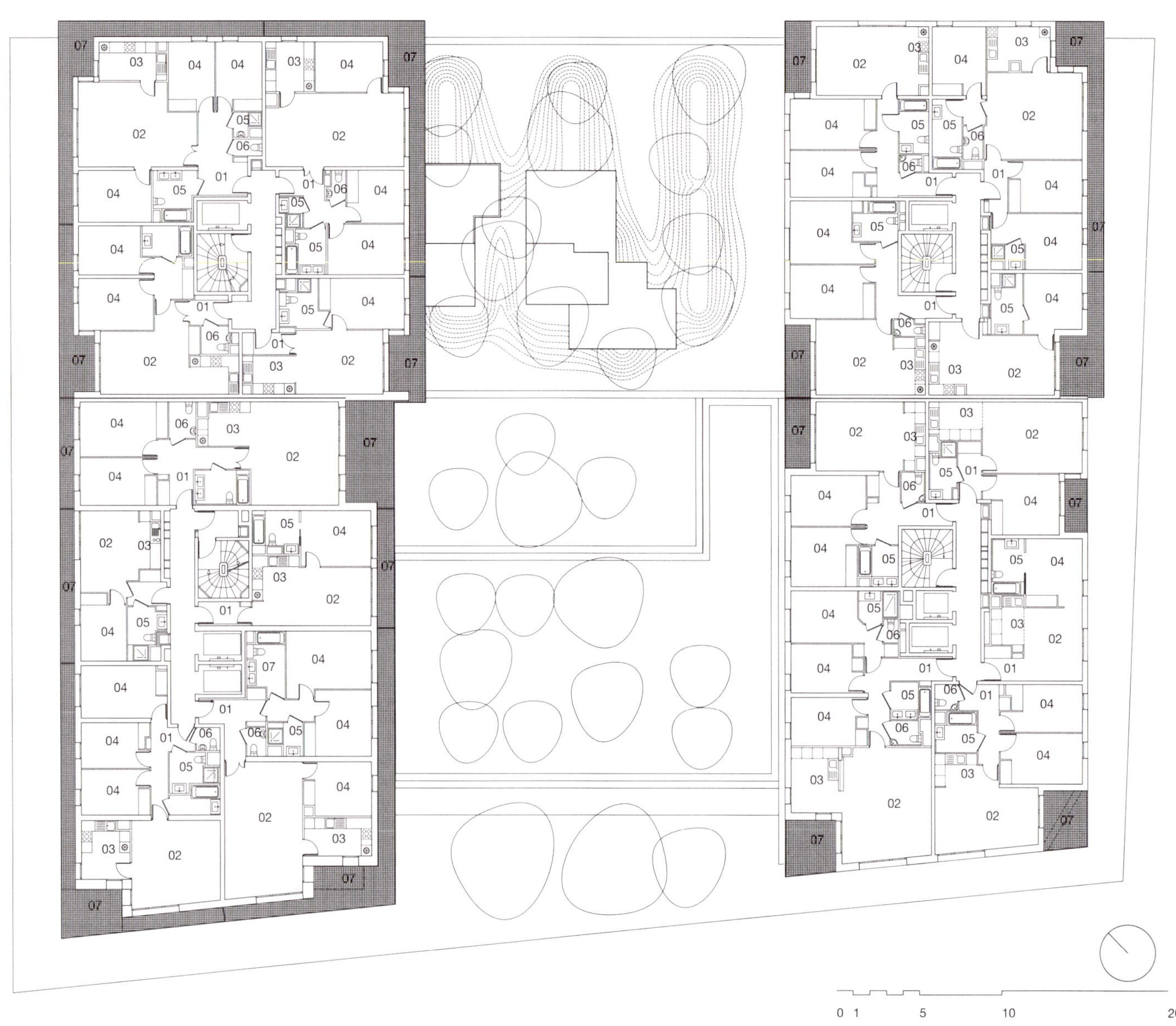

Sixth floor

Housing
01 Entrance hall
02 Living room
03 Kitchen
04 Bedroom
05 Bathroom
06 Restroom
07 Terrace-Loggia

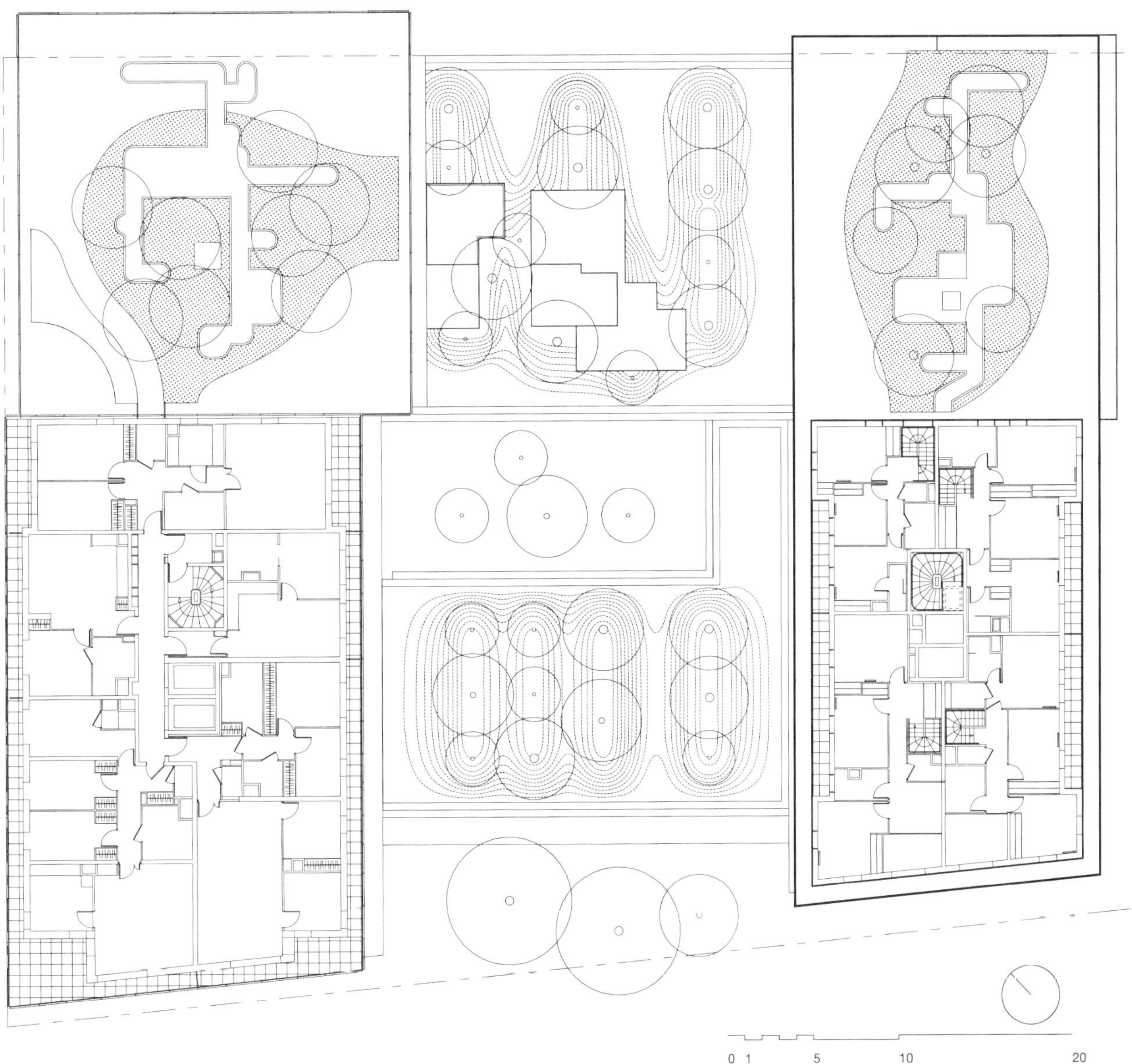

Tenth floor

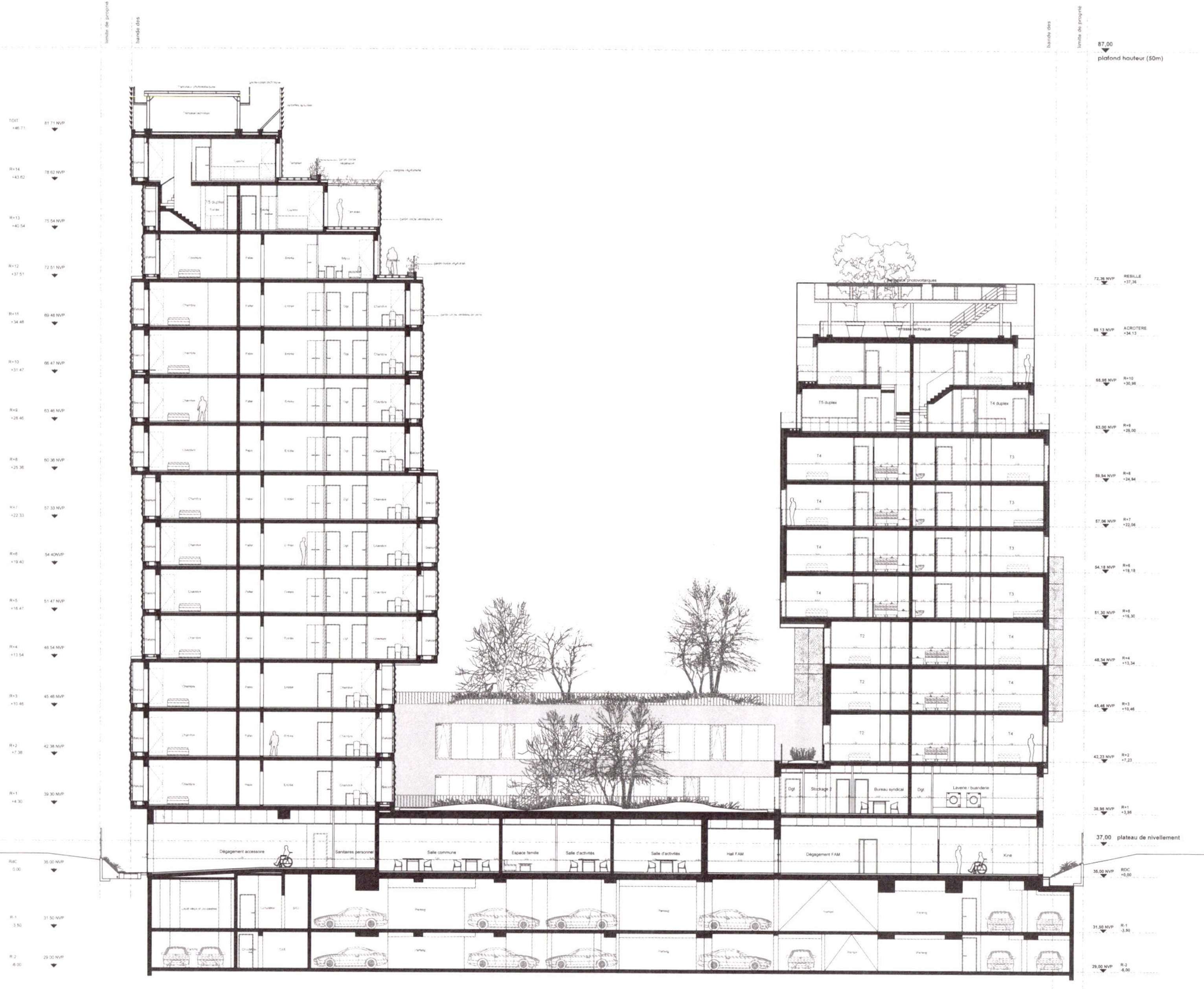

AA Section

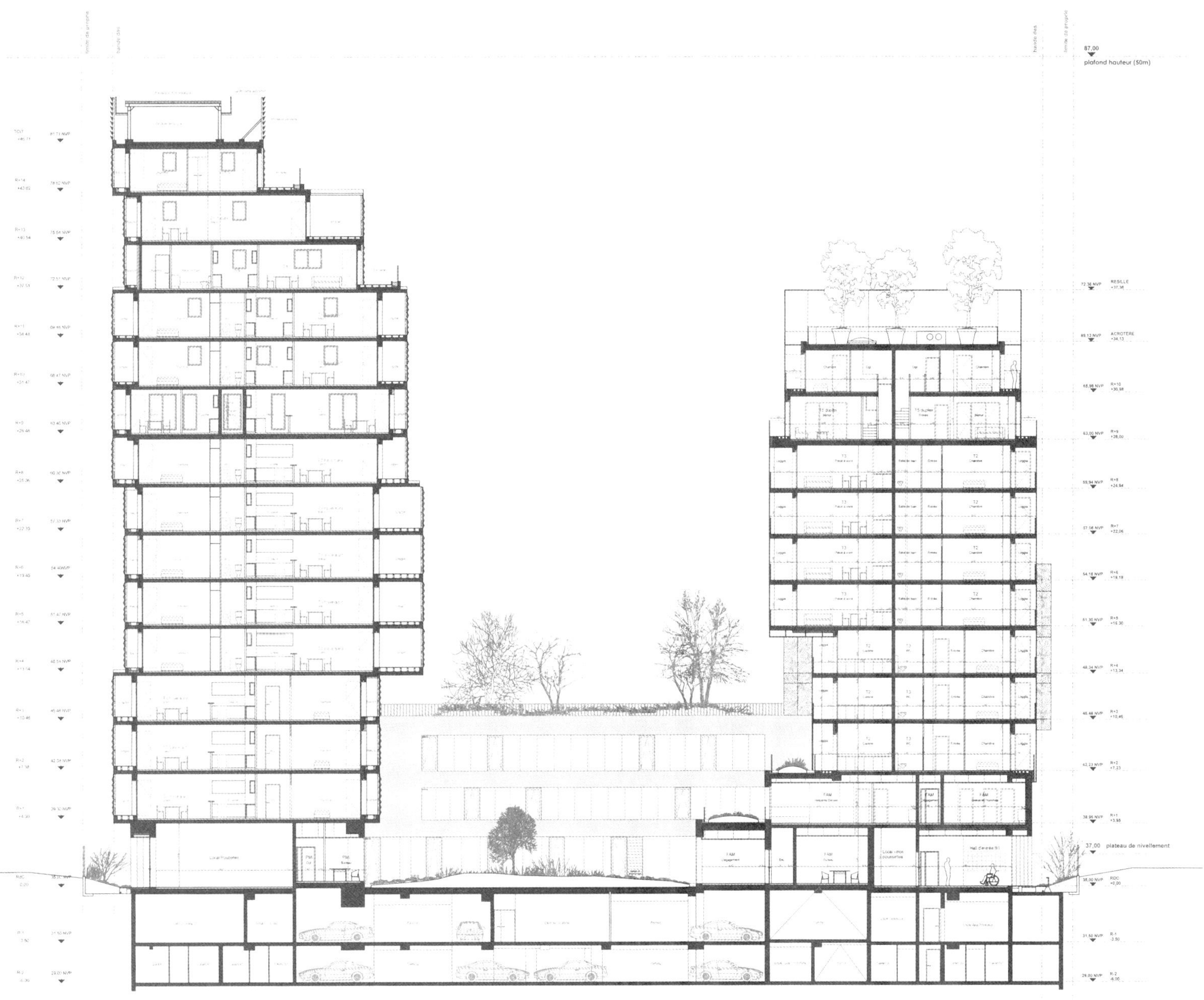

General cross-section

Construction Details

Building A construction drawings
Composition and adjustment of louvres

Gausa + Raveau actarquitectura

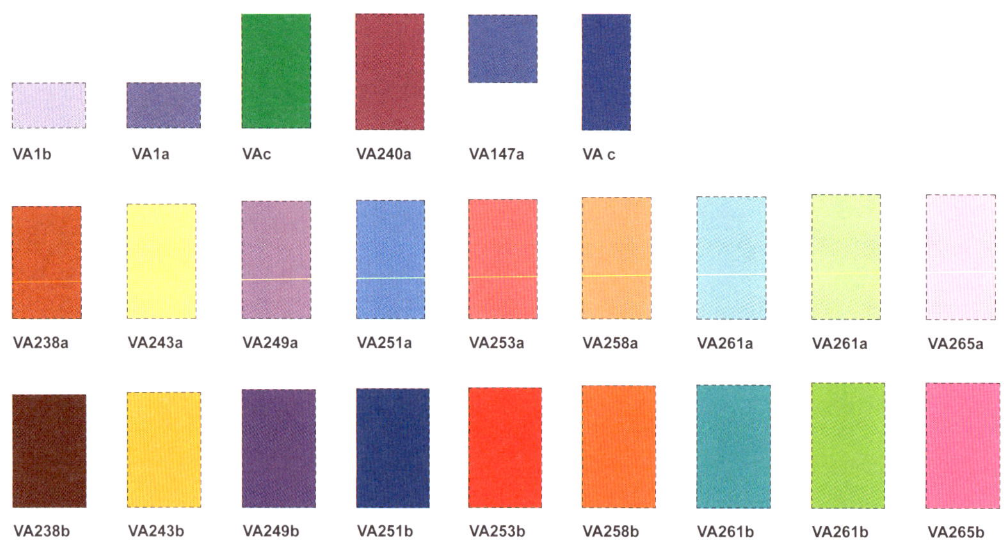

List of panels

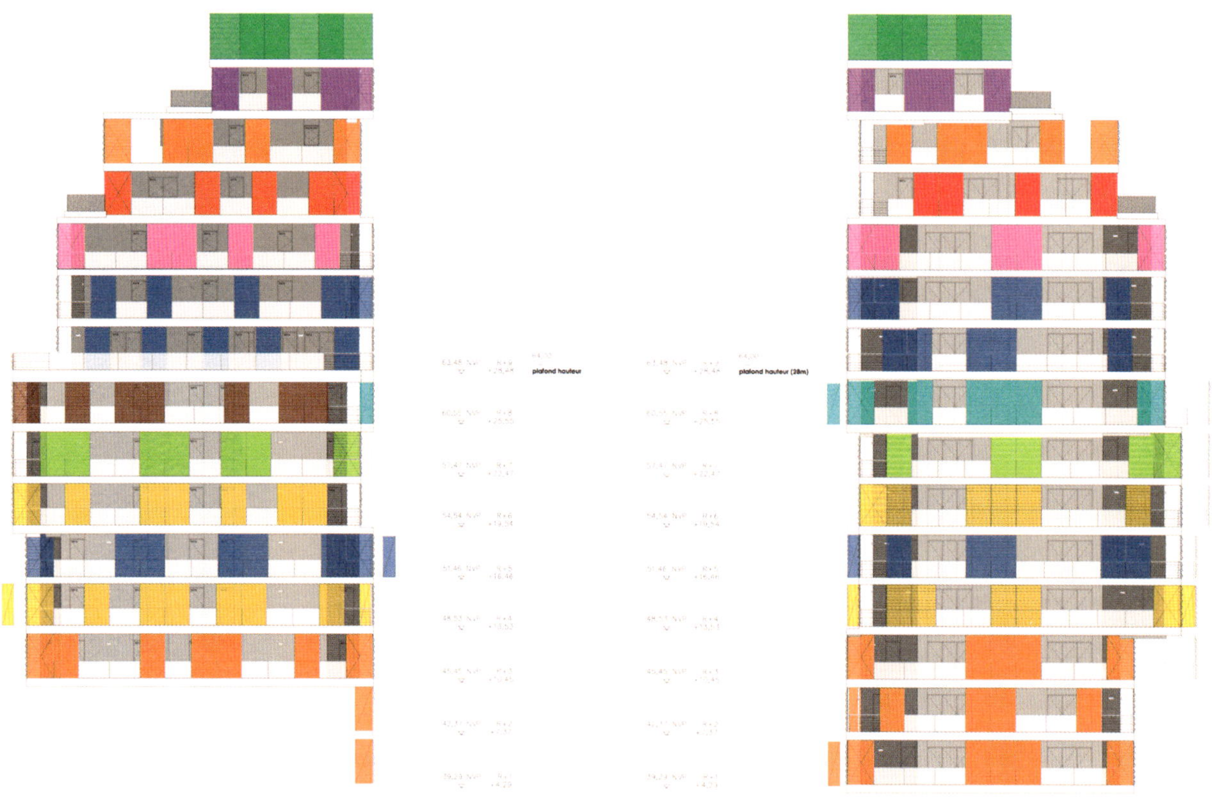

North-east facade

South-west facade

North-west facade

South-east facade

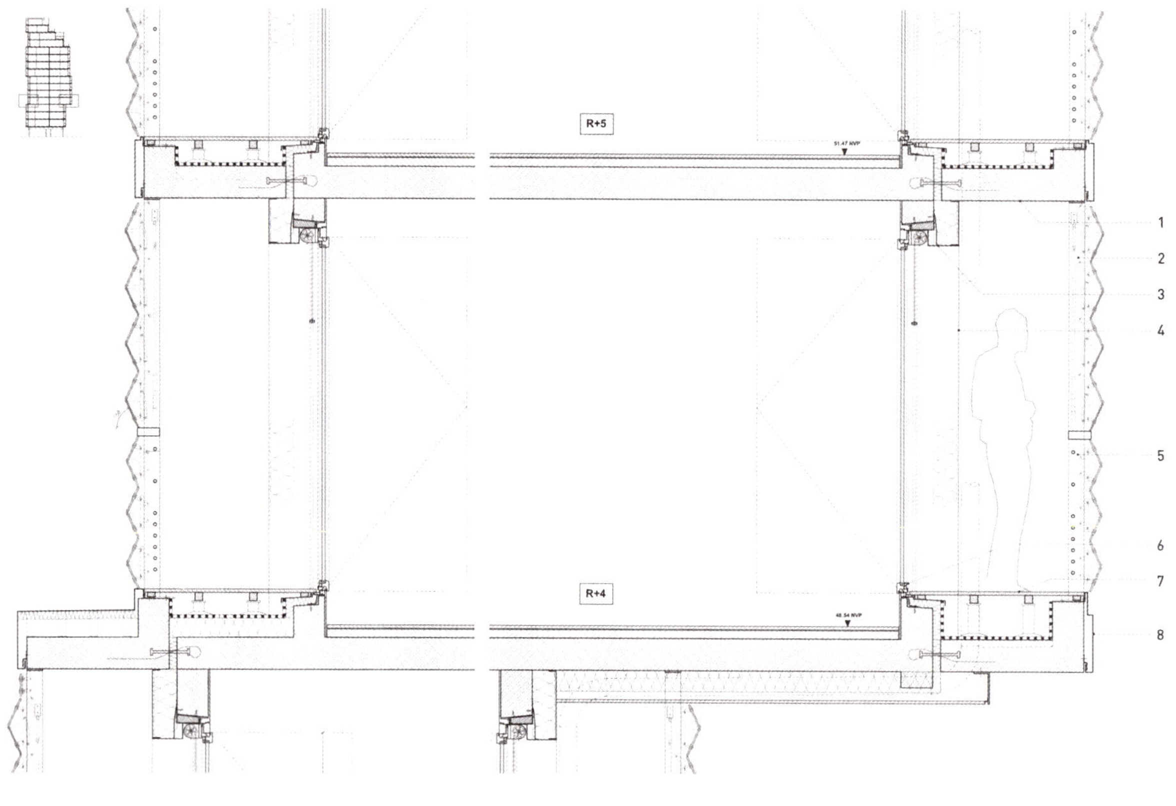

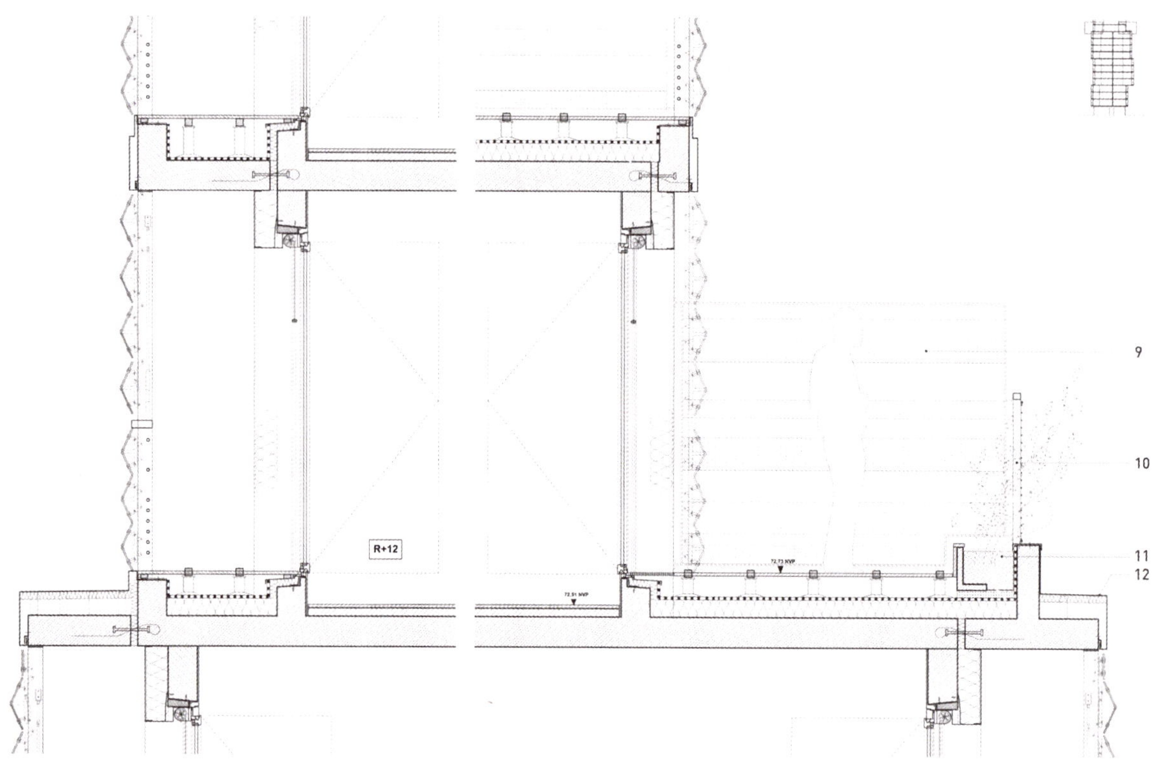

Balconies and loggia cross-sections

01 Balconies and loggia
02 Louvres facade
03 Patio door and blind
04 Masonry facade
05 Louvres safety panel
06 Slab edge cladding
07 Cladding to underside of balcony
08 Terrace
09 Screen
10 Safety panel
11 Planter
12 Ledge cladding

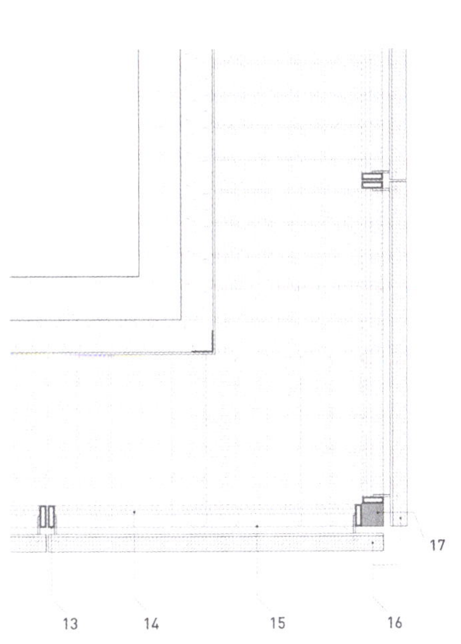

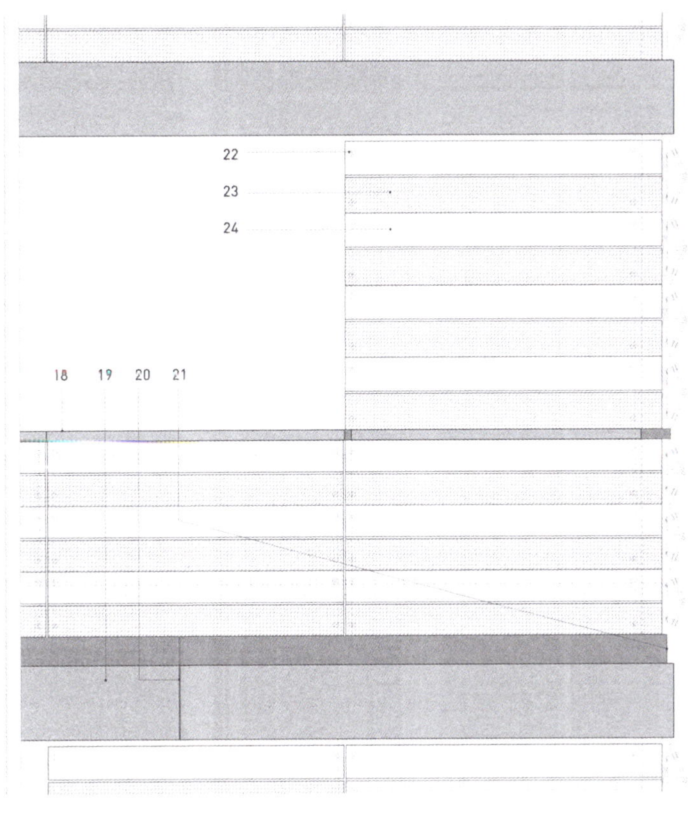

Balcony corner drawing

13 Half-height post: 30 x 100 mm
14 Horizontal edge: ⌀ 20 mm
15 Boundary of covering
16 Extended corner slats of 10 cm
17 Aluminium sheet cladding
18 Plain anodised aluminium handrail
19 Habillage nez de dalle tôle pliée aluminium anodisé naturel
20 Slab edge cladding: plain anodised folded aluminium sheet Joint min. (5 mm)
21 Special cutting out of the metal sheet
22 For corner joint
23 Slats tilted upwards: transparent laminated glass
24 Slats tilted downwards: reflective laminated glass

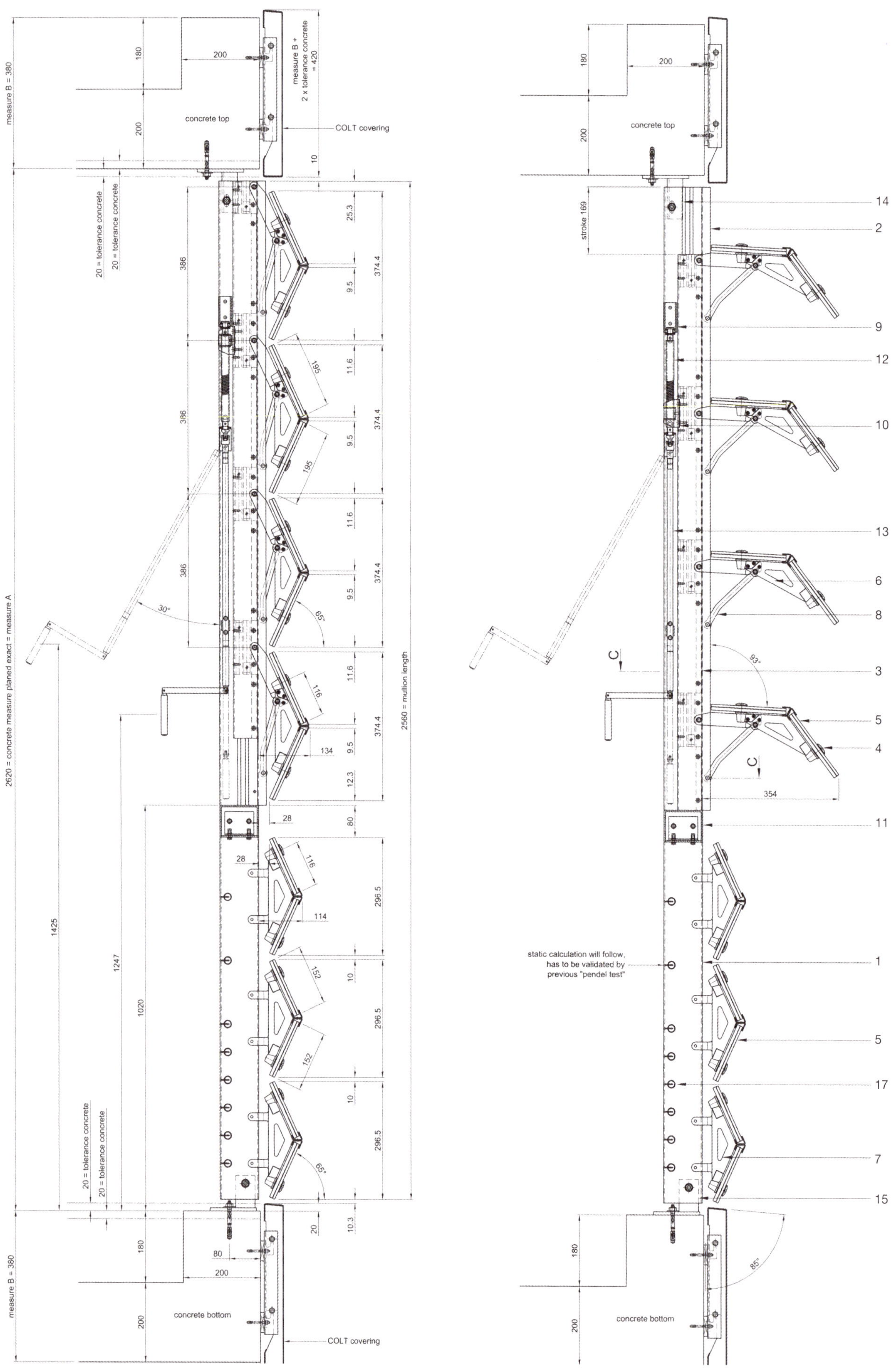

Principle vertical, section louvre closed/open

GOOD VIBRATIONS - CLICHY BATIGNOLLES

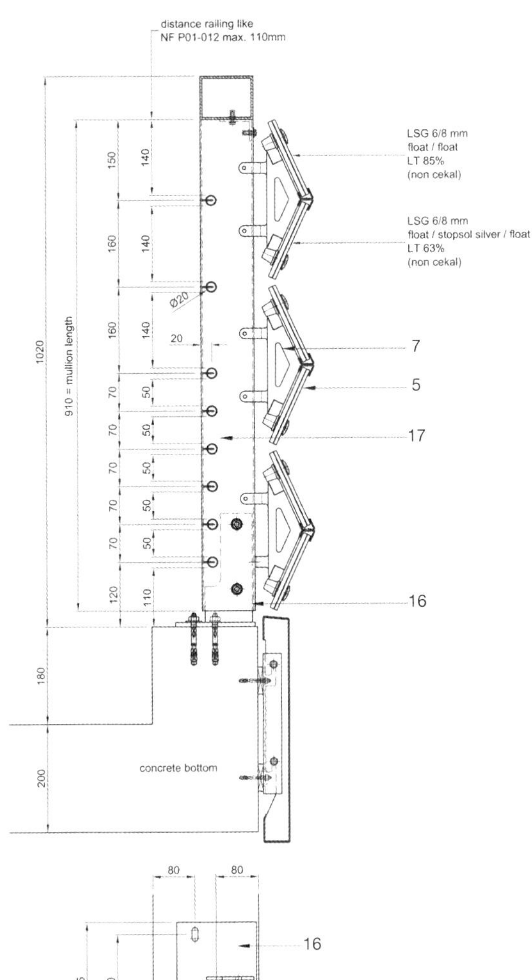

Principle vertical, section railing

item	description	material
1	mullion 100x40x3	Alu
2	mullion for control rod	Alu
3	control rod	Alu
4	point attachment	stainless steel
5	glass louvre 8 / 1,52 / 6mm	
6	glass holder movable louvre	Alu
7	glass holder fixed louvre	Alu
8	supporting arm	Alu
9	mullion bracket	stainless steel
10	control rod bracket	stainless steel
11	mullion horizontal 100x80	Alu
12	spindel shaft self locking	stainless steel
13	crank handle	Alu
14	bracket facade - mullion top	steel
15	bracket facade - mullion bottom 1	steel
16	bracket facade - mullion bottom 2	steel
17	railing	Alu

Glassholder fixed louvre for mock up screw or welded together

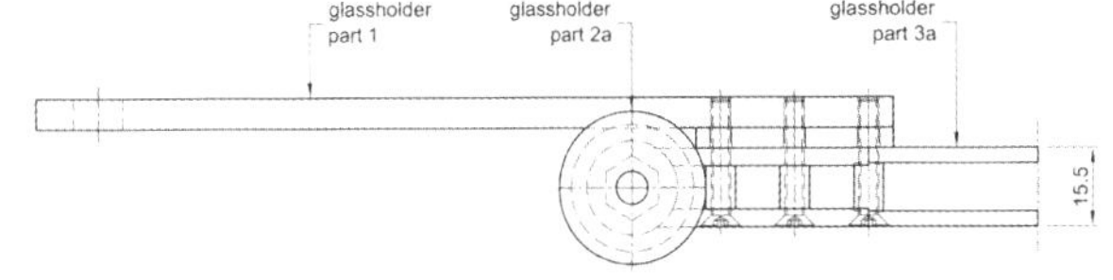

Section a, b, c glasholder

Building B construction drawings
Composition and adjustment of louvres

Avenier-Cornejo Architects

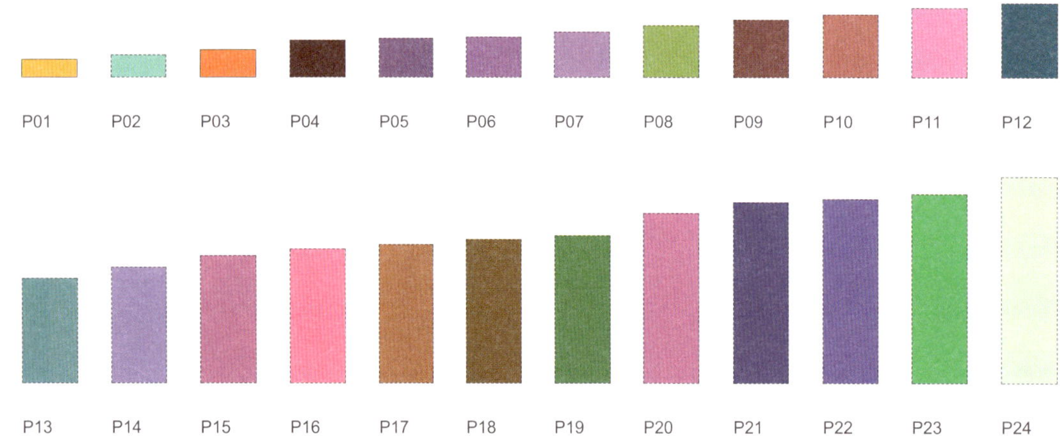

List of panels

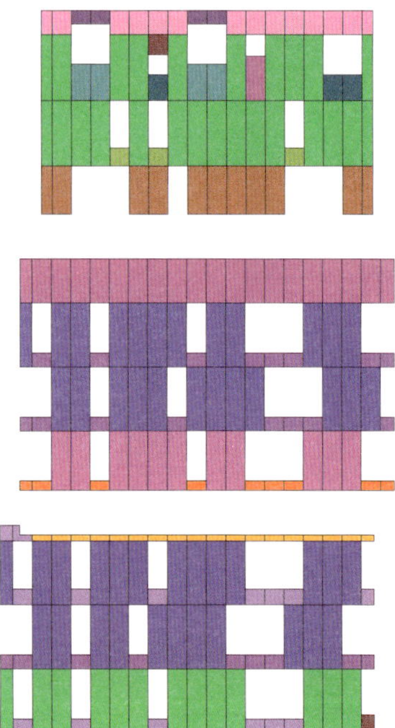

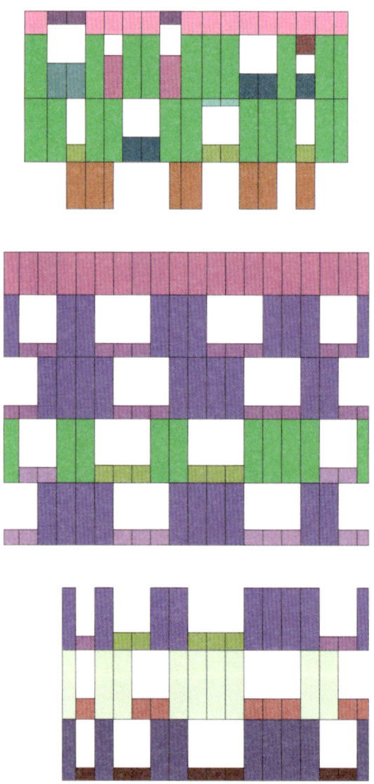

North-east facade

South-west facade

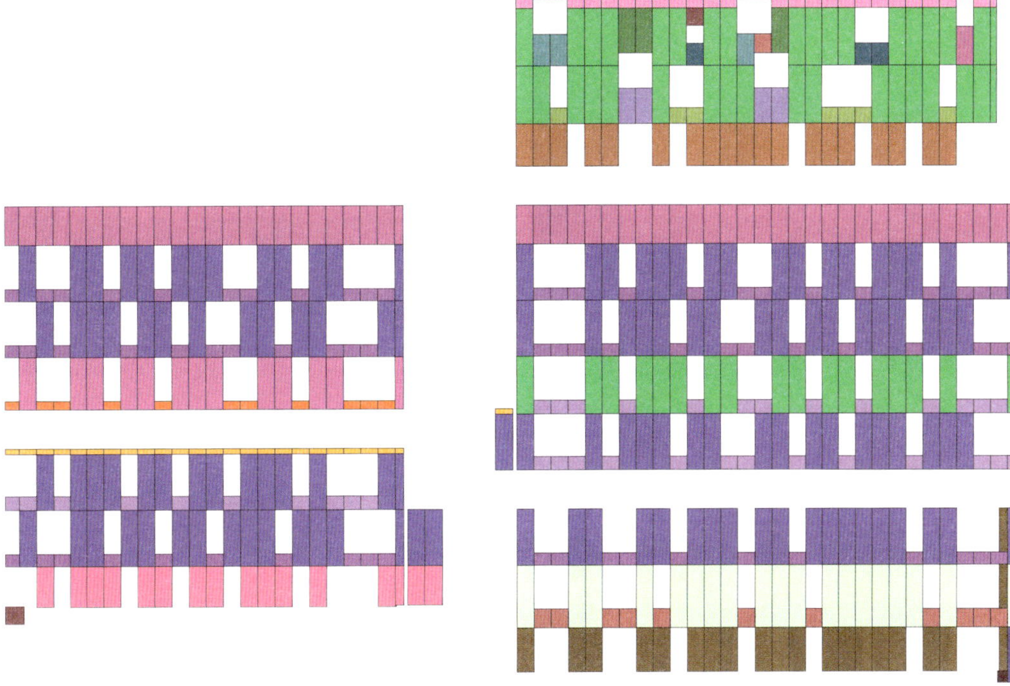

North-west facade

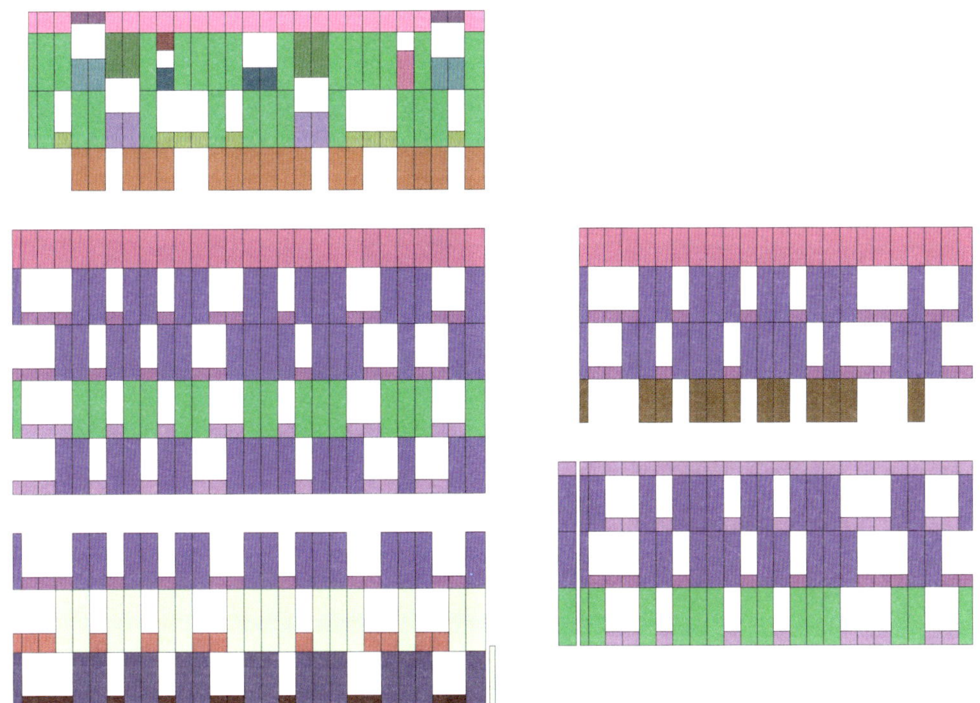

South-east facade

Elevation

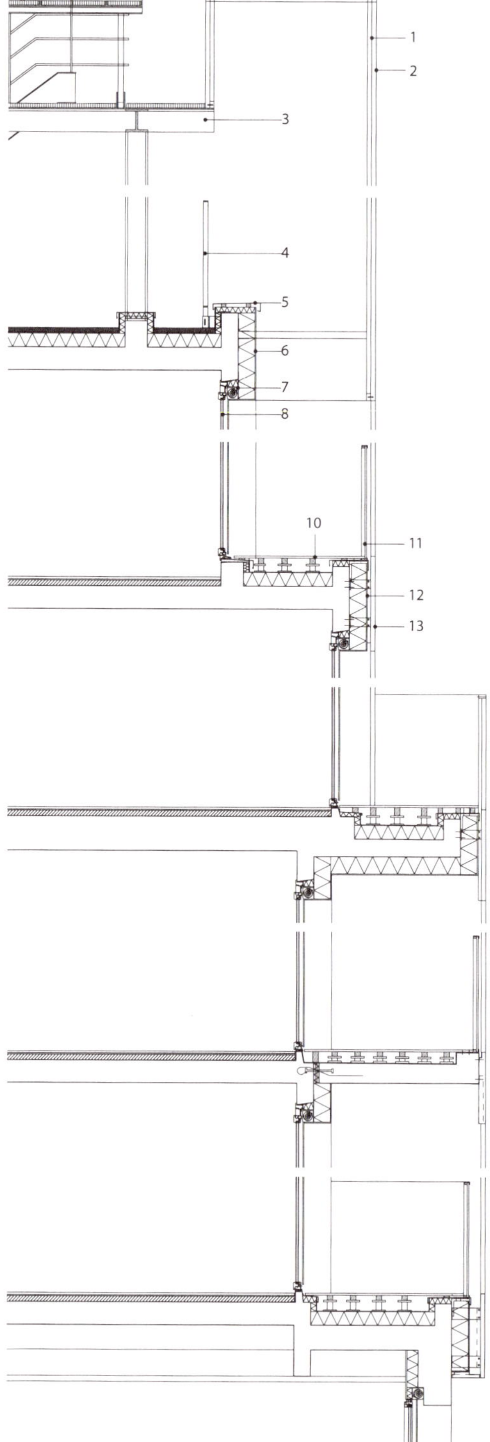

Facade cross-section detail

01 Metal framework for fixing white lacquered cladding
02 Perforated metal cladding folding onto the roof
03 White lacquered steel structural frame
04 Safety panel fixed to white lacquered steel bars
05 White lacquered aluminium capping
06 Light colour, fine floated render finish
07 Exterior facade blind with guide tracks
08 Aluminium/timber joinery
09 Lacquered aluminium sheet
10 Timber terrace on pads
11 Clear, laminated, toughened glazing fixed into rebates top and bottom
12 Waterproof breathable membrane
13 Perforated lacquered aluminium cladding

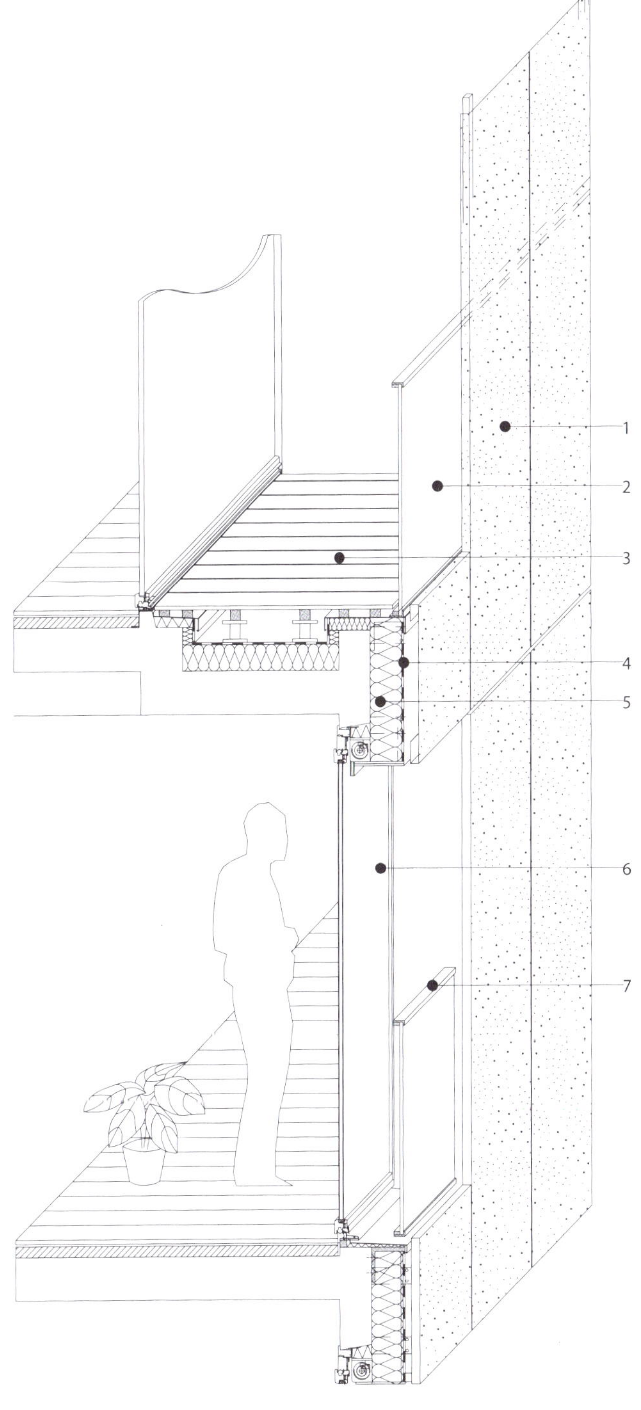

Axonometric view of balcony

01 Full-height cladding of white lacquered, perforated 30/10 steel
02 Glazed safety panel fixed into rebates top and bottom fixed to a continuous bracket
03 Timber decking up to the joinery
04 Waterproof breathable membrane
05 External insulation
06 Aluminium/timber joinery, inward opening casements
07 RAL lacquered steel at the choice of the architect

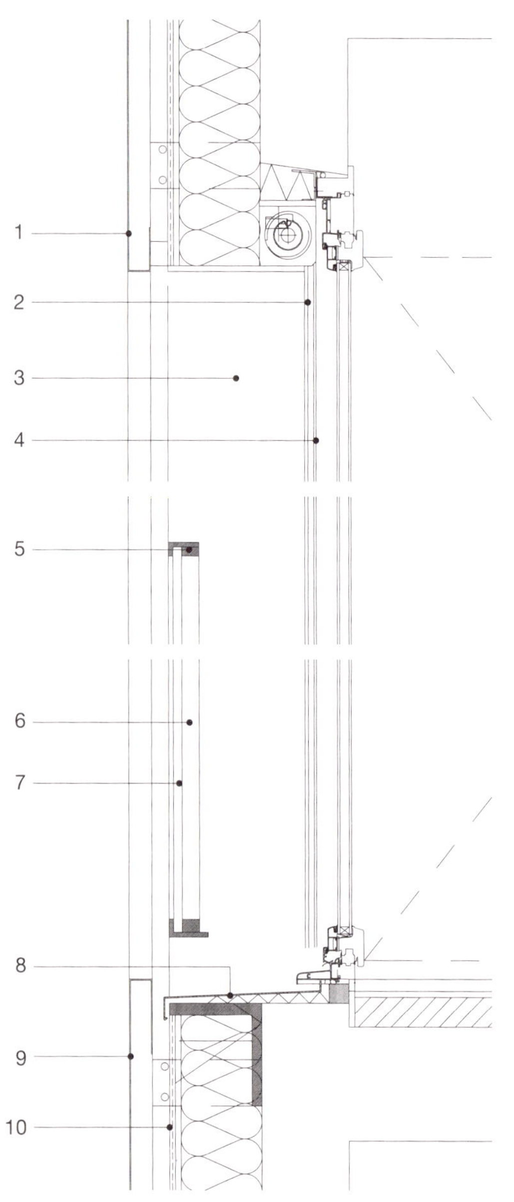

Window cross-section detail

01 Perforated lacquered aluminium cladding
02 Guide rail
03 Lacquered aluminium sheet
04 Aluminium/timber joinery, inward opening casements
05 Lacquered steel rails
06 Lacquered steel jamb
07 Glazing fixed into rebates top and bottom
08 Lacquered aluminium flashing behind cladding fixed to a continuous bracket
09 Metal framework for fixing cladding
10 Waterproof breathable membrane

Pattern 1

Perforation open rate 6 %

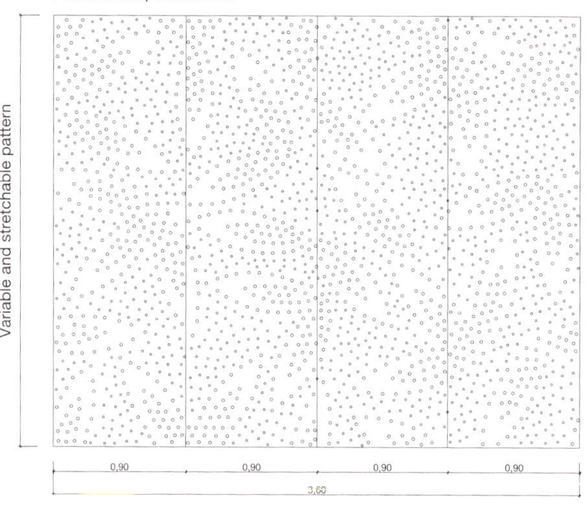

Pattern 2

Perforation open rate 15 %

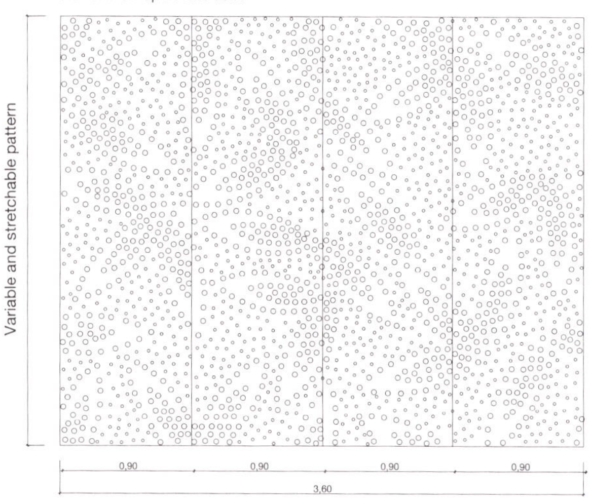

Pattern 5

Perforation open rate 23%

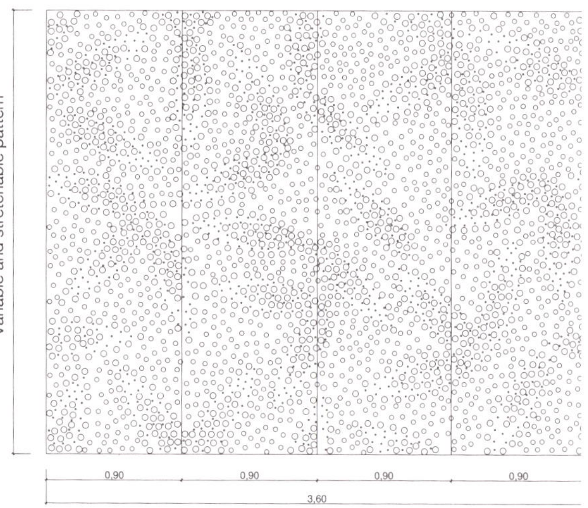

Facade patterns

Window elevation detail

01 Perforated, lacquered aluminium cladding, waterproof breathable membrane + insulation
02 Exterior facades blind with guide tracks
03 Aluminium/timber joinery, inward opening casements
04 Glazed safety panel with vertical steel rail fixed into rebates top and bottom

Window plan detail

01 Exterior facade blind with guide tracks
02 Concealed opening frame fixed into aluminium/timber rebates
03 Lacquered aluminium sheet
04 Glazed safety panel with vertical steel rail and fixed into rebates top and bottom. Vertical steel rail fixed into rebates top and bottom
05 Steel mullion behind glazing + silicon seals
06 Insulation
07 Metal framework for fixing cladding
08 Waterproof breathable membrane

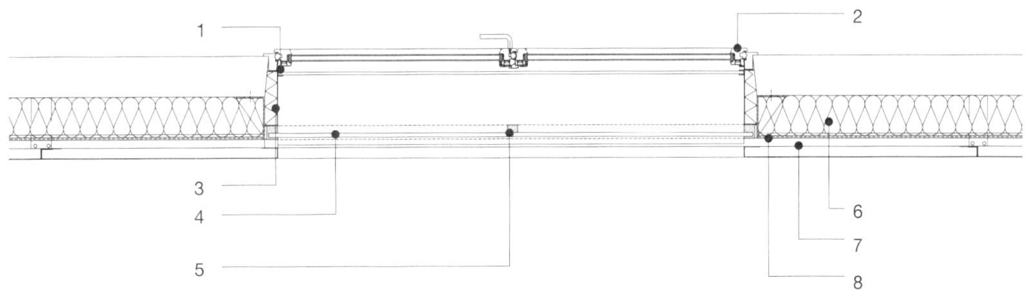

French Texts

TEXTES INSTITUTIONALS

Page 5_Fruit d'une collaboration heureuse entre les architectes Gausa + Raveau et Avenier Cornejo, le bâtiment E8 de la ZAC Clichy Batignolles illustre une promesse: celle que mon prédécesseur, Bertrand Delanoë, avait faite aux Parisiens lors de son arrivée en 2001, et celle que nous avons tenue en permettant à ce « morceau oublié » du territoire de se réinventer.

Promesse sociale d'abord, car le projet articule harmonieusement un programme mixte de 16 000 m² comprenant des logements en accession libre et d'autres à loyer maîtrisé, un foyer d'accueil médicalisé, un centre de protection maternelle infantile et un local d'activité. Promesse environnementale ensuite, car non content de produire de l'énergie, le bâtiment de 15 étages arbore des toitures végétalisées qui contribuent à son intégration dans l'environnement paysager du parc Martin-Luther-King.

Promesse architecturale enfin, car culminant à 50 mètres, l'édifice offre de nouvelles perspectives aux architectes pour construire le patrimoine de demain, et aux Parisiens pour investir l'espace qui leur revient.

Deux ans après son inauguration, l'immeuble s'est fondu dans le paysage comme dans le quotidien de ceux qui y résident, y travaillent ou passent devant chaque jour, conjuguant de façon ingénieuse les exigences d'une ville qui entend embrasser sa modernité: densité de population, qualité du cadre de vie et respect des normes environnementales en vigueur.

Incarnant le renouveau d'un quartier devenu « éco-quartier », d'une enclave ferroviaire muée en écosystème urbain, il est pour la ville de Paris un vibrant modèle de développement durable, et la preuve s'il en fallait qu'espagnols et français savent prendre de la hauteur.

Anne Hidalgo
Maire de Paris

Page 6_L'éco-quartier Clichy-Batignolles, dont la construction sera achevée en 2020, est l'un des projets urbains les plus ambitieux actuellement développés par la Ville de Paris. La qualité architecturale, qui fait naturellement partie de cette ambition, ne doit pas faire oublier les nombreux défis programmatiques, urbains et environnementaux relevés à chaque étape de sa conception et de sa réalisation.

Clichy-Batignolles est venu réemployer une enclave urbaine particulièrement contrainte par la présence d'infrastructures ferroviaires et routières. De superficie relativement modeste eu égard à son programme—plus de 500 000 m² de constructions à forte mixité programmatique—le site n'en a pas moins permis la création d'un parc public majeur, le parc Martin Luther King, qui aura 10 ha dans sa forme définitive. D'où la complexité d'un projet appelé à conjuguer ce grand espace ouvert avec une intensité urbaine forte. S'y ajoutent des objectifs environnementaux très ambitieux, notamment en termes de maîtrise de l'énergie, le quartier visant la neutralité carbone.

Conçu par l'urbaniste François Grether et la paysagiste Jacqueline Osty le grand parc central est un élément clé. Il est à la fois une pièce maîtresse de la trame verte du Nord-Ouest parisien, un espace de liaison entre des quartiers riverains autrefois séparés, une destination de loisirs pour tous et le paysage sur lequel ouvrent nombre de fenêtres de l'éco-quartier. On ne peut manquer sa présence depuis les rues périphériques, où elle se diffuse par des espaces végétalisés et se perçoit à travers pas moins de 14 entrées. Les constructions prennent place non pas autour, mais sur le pourtour de ce parc, sans rupture physique.

Le Lot E8 est particulièrement représentatif de trois aspects structurants du projet Clichy-Batignolles. Le premier est justement ce rapport intime au pawrc, qui vient le border sur trois côtés. Le second est sa forte mixité programmatique, avec des logements de différents types, mais aussi un foyer d'accueil médicalisé, un centre de protection maternelle et infantile et des commerces. Le troisième est sa hauteur : en application d'une disposition spécifique du règlement d'urbanisme parisien, le Lot E8 est l'un des 8 immeubles du projet dont la hauteur avoisine 50 m, et le premier à être construit (le régime général plafonne la hauteur à 30 m).

De volume important, le Lot E8 a été délimité pour permettre la construction d'un couple d'immeubles, afin précisément de maîtriser au mieux ces trois enjeux, par une conception faisant appel à deux équipes d'architectes. Le résultat est à la hauteur des attentes de l'aménageur et de la Ville de Paris. Le parc entre généreusement dans la faille qui traverse en son centre l'îlot dessiné par Gausa & Raveau et Avenier & Cornejo Architectes. Les équipements médico-sociaux y sont à la fois ouverts sur l'extérieur et à l'abri des regards. Les toitures terrasses végétalisées viennent parfaire l'intégration du projet dans le paysage du parc.

Quant à la hauteur, la dissymétrie et les effets de déhanchement horizontaux la font oublier au profit d'une impression d'élégante légèreté. Pour un projet qui, sur ce point très sensible à Paris, avait valeur de test, la réussite est indéniable.

Jean-François Danon
Directeur général de la société publique locale Paris Batignolles Aménagement

Page 7_Sur près de 54 hectares, l'écoquartier de Clichy Batignolles, comprenant l'opération que nous avons développée avec notre partenaire Linkcity, constitue un lieu singulier, au carrefour de plusieurs quartiers parisiens et au cœur du quartier central des affaires de La Défense et de la Plaine Saint-Denis.

Reconversion urbaine d'un nouvel ordre, ce quartier incarne en effet l'engagement du Grand Paris en matière de développement durable, en étant à l'avant-garde de problématiques urbaines phares telles que l'utilisation d'énergies renouvelables, la gestion de l'eau ou encore celle des déchets. Le quartier constitue une interface privilégiée avec la nature en plein Paris. Ici, l'aménagement paysager participe à la biodiversité urbaine sur près de 10 hectares en liaison avec le Parc Martin Luther King. Pour notre Groupe, fortement engagé pour la qualité de vie en ville et la création de solutions urbaines durables, participer au renouvellement urbain du Nord-Ouest parisien et créer une solution urbaine exemplaire constituait une grande ambition. Et c'est avec passion que nous avons imaginé un programme remarquable, visant une réelle mixité programmatique, en cohérence avec l'écoquartier dans lequel il s'insère.

Ce projet initié en 2013, totalise 27 mois de travaux. Il conjugue le savoir-faire Cogedim, offrant à ses résidents une réelle exigence architecturale au service de la qualité de vie. Constitué de deux bâtiments, cet ensemble d'une surface totale de 16 000 m² est le premier immeuble de 50 mètres de hauteur de l'opération Clichy-Batignolles. Les architectes Gausa + Raveau et Avenier & Cornejo signent une conception en hauteur graduelle, qui tire le meilleur parti du parc Marin Luther King qui l'entoure en offrant une vue dégagée sur le parc pour la plupart des logements.

Nous avons mobilisé le savoir-faire du groupe Altarea Cogedim, pour répondre à l'évolution de ce quartier et anticiper les attentes des résidents et des utilisateurs qui aujourd'hui travaillent dans les locaux d'activité, comme celui de la PMI, que nous avons aussi réalisés. Les lignes architecturales contemporaines sont conçues au service du bien-être et du confort de tous les habitants.

Fiers d'avoir été associés à ce programme ambitieux, dans un secteur stratégique et dynamique de la capitale, nous agissons envers les territoires en entreprise responsable. Cet engagement sociétal nous le défendons sur tous nos programmes afin d'offrir plus de mieux vivre en ville. Et il se traduit ici par notre la volonté d'agir pour la mixité urbaine, sociale et programmatique.

Laurence Beardsley
Président, Cogedim Paris Métropole

Page 9_Le projet Clichy-Batignolles
Sur 54 hectares dans le 17e arrondissement de Paris, le projet Clichy-Batignolles est de par son ampleur et ses ambitions, l'un des plus grands projets urbains mené à Paris. Conçu pour relier et valoriser les quartiers qui l'entourent, Clichy-Batignolles est d'abord un grand parc au nord-ouest de Paris, naturel et traversant, dont près de 7 hectares (sur 10 à terme) sont d'ores et déjà ouverts au public. Autour de cet espace exceptionnel s'organise un quartier ouvert et mixte, conjuguant toutes les composantes de la ville (logements pour tous, bureaux, commerces, équipements et espaces publics), qui accueillera à terme 7.500 habitants et 12.700 emplois.

Terrain d'application privilégié des ambitions de la Ville de Paris en faveur d'un urbanisme durable, les objectifs environnementaux assignés au quartier sont particulièrement exigeants. La sobriété énergétique et le recours aux énergies renouvelables (géothermie alimentant le réseau de chauffage et d'eau chaude sanitaire et production d'électricité à partir de panneaux photovoltaïques) permettent de tendre vers un bilan carbone neutre du quartier. Clichy Batignolles est également en pointe dans la mise en œuvre du plan biodiversité grâce en particulier au parc Martin Luther King, inscrit dans la trame verte du nord-ouest parisien.

Sur le plan résidentiel, l'opération contribue de manière significative à la production de logements puisque 3.400 logements sont livrés ou en cours de réalisation, dont au moins 50% de logements sociaux et 20% de logement locatifs intermédiaires avec des réponses adaptées à la diversité des besoins (étudiants, personnes âgées dépendantes, jeunes actifs, résidence doctorante…)

Le renforcement de la desserte en transport en commun est l'une des conditions d'un développement équilibré et durable de ce territoire. A l'horizon d'achèvement de l'opération, la ligne 14 du métro et le tramway T3 prolongés s'ajoutant à la desserte existante par le transilien, le RER C et la ligne 13 du métro, feront de Clichy Batignolles l'un des quartiers les mieux desservis de la métropole. Les ambitions pour ce quartier se lisent aussi dans la tour emblématique de 160 mètres de haut conçue par Renzo Piano pour le palais de justice de Paris, tout comme dans la conception architecturale des programmes qui s'attache à tirer le meilleur parti du parc et des possibilités nouvelles, offertes ici, de construire des immeubles de logements pouvant atteindre 50 mètres.

La réalisation de l'opération Clichy-Batignolles, lancée en 2002, est aujourd'hui largement engagée. En rive du parc, le long de l'avenue de Clichy, 1 516 logements, deux groupes scolaires, une crèche, un foyer d'accueil médicalisé, une PMI et 3 300 m² de commerces et services, ont été livrés. Les réalisations se succèdent dorénavant à un rythme soutenu conduisant à l'achèvement de l'opération à l'horizon 2020.

L'éco-quartier
Labellisé Nouveau Quartier Urbain par la région Île-de-France, Clichy-Batignolles est l'un des éco-quartiers par lesquels la Ville de Paris met en œuvre une politique ambitieuse de développement durable, exprimée notamment par son Plan Climat et son Plan Biodiversité.

La Ville de Paris a adopté récemment un Plan Biodiversité dont Clichy-Batignolles constitue une préfiguration pour ce qui concerne les opérations d'aménagement. Dans le parc Martin Luther King, une faune et une flore particulièrement riches se développent autour d'un fossé humide et d'un bassin biotope. Le parc s'insère dans une trame verte composée du Parc Monceau, du Bois de Boulogne, de plusieurs squares (dont ceux des Batignolles et des Épinettes) ainsi que des cimetières de Montmartre et de Clichy. Cette trame verte constituera un atout majeur pour le maintien de la biodiversité à Paris. Hormis le parc proprement dit, la protection et le développement de la biodiversité passent par les plantations variées le long des voiries, les cœurs d'îlot paysagés et les toitures végétalisées. Les cahiers de prescriptions environnementales imposent des coefficients de biodiversité calculés à partir de la végétalisation des surfaces horizontales et verticales des projets.

Le Lot E8
Sur plus de 16 000 m² de surface de plancher, le programme du Lot E8 de l'opération Clichy-Batignolles a été remporté par le groupement Altarea-Cogedim/Linkcity Ile-de-France. Entamés en juillet 2013, les travaux ont duré 27 mois. Conçu par l'équipe d'architectes Gausa + Raveau et Avenier & Cornejo, il se compose d'un ensemble mixte constitué de :
– 62 logements à loyers maîtrisés réalisés par Linkcity Ile-de-France pour le compte d'ICF Novedis ;
– 83 logements en accession libre réalisés par

Altarea-Cogedim pour le compte de la Caisse Autonome de Retraite des Chirurgiens Dentiste et des Sages-Femmes;
– Un foyer d'accueil médicalisé de 40 lits et 6 places d'accueil de jour réalisés par Linkcity Ile-de-France pour le compte de RSF;
– Un centre de consultation PMI, réalisés par Linkcity Ile-de-France pour le compte du Département de Paris;
– Un local d'activité réalisé par Linkcity Ile-de-France pour le compte de SDIC.

Les ambitions architecturales du programme s'expriment par la réalisation d'un ensemble mixte constitué de quatre bâtiments allant de R+9 à R+14, sur un socle commun. S'inscrivant dans la continuité des lots déjà réalisés sur le secteur Est de la ZAC, le Lot E8 a la particularité d'être le premier programme livré de logements de la ZAC atteignant 50 mètres, s'élevant ainsi sur 15 étages. Cette opération s'attache à tirer le meilleur parti du parc Martin-Luther-King et des possibilités nouvelles, offertes ici, de conjuguer densité et cadre de vie. La répartition des programmes de logements en deux lots de hauteur graduelle ménage une large perspective depuis l'intérieur de l'îlot et permet d'offrir une vue dégagée sur le parc à la plupart des logements. Des toitures végétalisées contribuent à l'intégration du projet dans l'environnement paysager du parc Martin-Luther-King et offrent des espaces de détente aux résidents. L'ensemble se caractérise par une forte présence du verre et de résilles métalliques perforées blanches pour habiller les façades.

Le Lot E8 respecte les prescriptions environnementales particulièrement exigeantes de l'opération Clichy Batignolles et produit 44MWh/an . Il est certifié H&E – Profil A option Performance et labellisé BBC Effinergie.

Batignolles 08
Le nouveau quartier Clichy-Batignolles appartient au grand paysage ouvert de la ceinture verte et fait le lien entre les différents quartiers du 17e arrondissement. Dans ce dispositif, Batignolles O8 est emblématique, à la jonction des grandes lignes qui façonnent ce territoire : voie nord-sud, boulevard Berthier, voies ferroviaires, parc Martin Luther King. Il bénéficie d'un potentiel extraordinaire de centralité, fédérateur d'usages et de lien social.

Batignolles 08 est une opération multi-produits d'envergure réalisée par Linkcity Ile-de-France et Nexity. Elle est remarquable par sa complexité qui s'exprime par l'imbrication de nombreux programmes. En effet, le projet se compose de 80 logements à loyer maitrisé, 153 logements locatifs sociaux, 72 logements vendus en accession libre à la propriété, 42 logements vendus en usufruit locatif social, mais aussi un centre d'animation, un cinéma de 7 salles ainsi que des commerces en pied d'immeuble.

Le Lot 08 s'articule autour de trois bâtiments de 50 mètres de hauteur avec plusieurs programmes de logements bénéficiant de larges terrasses ou de balcons, d'un pôle culture et loisirs composé d'un ensemble de commerces, d'un centre d'animation réalisé pour la Ville de Paris avec une salle de concert et d'un cinéma.

La morphologie du projet a été réfléchie de manière à limiter les masques sur les projets voisins (Lots 06B, 07 et 09). Les architectes de l'opération, les agences Trévelo Viger Kohler et Tolila +Gilliland, ont également souhaité un prolongement du parc à l'intérieur du lot de manière à assurer sa bonne intégration dans l'environnement de la ZAC.

Batignolles O8 est un projet complexe, caractérisé par une forte imbrication des programmes, une densité élevée, une mixité des usages et des typologies de logements et par l'intervention de nombreux acteurs que Linkcity Ile-de-France a su faire travailler de concert.

A propos de Linkcity Ile-de-France
Depuis 30 ans, la société s'attache à développer des projets immobiliers innovants et différenciants, de toute nature pour le compte d'utilisateurs ou d'investisseurs publics ou privés. Elle s'affirme en tant qu'acteur majeur en matière de projets urbains et d'aménagement des territoires.

Acteur urbain engagé dans la construction de la métropole du Grand Paris, Linkcity Ile-de-France développe avec ses partenaires et pour ses clients de nouveaux quartiers de vie. Pour exemple, elle démarrera la construction du premier quartier zéro carbone, « Ilot Fertile » à Paris, début 2019.

Linkcity Ile-de-France développe également des opérations immobilières clés en main, des opérations de rénovation ou de constructions neuves. Pour exemple, elle réalise actuellement la Tour Alto à Paris La Défense.

Loïc Madeline
Directeur Général Délégué LinkCity

PRÉFACE
Page 10_ **Osciller, vibrer, résonner**
Manuel Gausa

L'opération L8 donne réponse à un programme riche –et exemplaire– de mixité urbaine: un ensemble de 160 logements (en accession et maîtrisés) divisés en deux corps construits situés sur un grand socle médical et social, face au nouveau et vibrant parc Martin Luther King, dans la ZAC Clichy Batignolles.

Depuis le début nous avons été conscients, en tant qu´architectes responsables de la Maîtrise d´Ouvrage, d'être devant un site particulier et exceptionnel: un site inscrit dans la systématique des grands parcs et ZACS périphériques, autour de la ville de Paris et qui parle, de fait, d'un changement d'échelle et de musique urbaines –ou de rythme, si l´on veut– dans ce grand lieu-nœud (juste le contraire de tout ce que pourrait être un non-lieu) qui veut être un espace de transfert, collectif et connectif, entre mailles et tissus, entre infrastructures et éco-structures, entre espaces construits et espaces verts, entre vides et pleins, entre pulsions urbaines et interactions citoyennes; un grand scénario diversifié de croisements et d'entrelacements entre échelles, trames et horizons, appelé à réunir convivialité domestique et dynamisme urbain).
La volonté du projet a été, depuis le début, celle de travailler avec des mouvements dans l'espace plus qu´avec des volumétries. Avec des mouvements subtils –rythmés, résonnants– plus qu´avec des volumétries trop figées ou monolithiques.

Mouvements susceptibles de « bouger » et de « vibrer » avec les différents rythmes du contexte et en même temps de pondérer – voire d'équilibrer – les différentes hauteurs existantes ou prévues dans le site. Mouvements de va et vient, de flux et reflux, qui tâcheraient de combiner l´idée de poussée verticale et l´idée de vibration horizontale.

Comme si la ville oscillait dans cet emplacement. Toute l´opération proposée pourrait être décrite par ces mouvements de glissement et de déplacement, en plan et en hauteur, de quatre corps, accolés et/ou accouplés deux à deux, qui s´élèvent séparés par un grand espace «vide» central.

Une stratégie qui permettrait, d´un côté, de répondre avec efficacité aux gabarits prévus dans le PLU et dans le cahier de charges (en s´adaptant par des retraits successifs à la ligne des 45° normative); qui primerait, de l´autre, la substitution de l´idée de l´îlot fermé ou semi-fermé par celle de l´îlot traversant, mettant en valeur l´importance de cette idée de percée, orientée du parc vers l´intérieur, susceptible d´unir, avec des liaisons frontales et diagonales à la fois:
– le parc et les tissus intérieurs,
– les espaces avant et les espaces arrière,
– les îlots frontaux et les îlots postérieurs,
– les nouveaux volumes et les anciennes trames, à travers cette ouverture centrale conjuguée avec celle autre latérale générée, à son tour, par la petite ceinture.

Une logique de glissements et de déplacements courtois qui, en plan masse, recueillent, par un léger retrait «poli», la présence de l'Hôtel Ibis et surtout la force-vecteur du nouveau bâtiment de Francis Soler, avec lequel le nouveau ensemble tâche d´établir un certain dialogue complice.

Mais aussi avec les autres îlots comme celui de TOA ou celui de PÉRIPHÉRIQUES, en primant une certaine idée de transition rythmée faite d´accords, d´alternances et de répliques (dans les grandeurs, les dimensions, dans les ouvertures, dans les couleurs et les textures...)

Dans ces corps qui bougent entre préexistences, cotoyances et connivences. Nous ne voulons pas de confrontations édiles mais de clins d´oeil amicaux entre différentes «fabriques urbaines».

En définitive, notre proposition veut primer une approche cohérente et en même temps différentielle ou la diversité serait obtenue non pas par addition ou par agrégation mais par déclinaison, par variation, d´une même logique commune: une logique capable de conjuguer l´idée de poussé et l´idée de trame; la dimension horizontale (du parc) et la force verticale (des émergences); à partir de l'évolution séquencée de ces quatre corps accouplés deux à deux qui:
– répondent à un même genre de formation et de géométrie
– partagent un même socle équipé
– s'élèvent avec des hauteurs variables, séparés par un grand vide central
– intègrent et expriment en façade, de façon propre et caractérisée dans chaque binôme, soit un programme de logements « en accession/élévation » (avec des rythmes plus saccadés et vibrants, avec des reflets miroités, plus changeants) soit un programme de logements plus « maîtrisé » (avec des mouvements plus lents, calmes et reposés, avec des surfaces plus lisses et opaques).

Une stratégie qui, d'un côté, permet de répondre avec efficacité aux gabarits prévus dans le site, de jouer sensiblement avec le contexte, de répondre avec précision et flexibilité à la mixité prévue et de privilégier une transversalité généreuse, « à travers », capable d'assurer à son tour une bonne illumination et orientation ainsi qu´une ventilation et un ensoleillement optimisés dans tout l'ensemble, et de ce fait, de favoriser des hautes qualités environnementales.

Nous avons défendu plus d´une fois que la « courtoisie urbaine » devrait substituer la simple accumulation iconique. Que la résonnance, la synergie, l´interaction entre informations, sollicitations, situations et conditions (mais aussi entre formulations et formations urbaines, entre signes et signaux) devrait proclamer un nouveau temps plus empathique et relationnel où la « dignité de vivre –la grande conquête du XXème siècle–se combinerait aujourd´hui avec le plaisir de vivre et de convivre.

Et cela à travers d´une architecture et d´un urbanisme plus interactifs, en interaction positive, globale et locale, avec la ville (multiple) et avec le contexte (unique); avec l´environnement (sensible) et avec la technologie (performative); avec la société (de chaque temps) et avec la culture et la création (du propre temps).

Manuel Gausa, Docteur architecte, Chaire d'urbanisme, Université de Gênes

---

ZOOM OUT
Page 16_ **Les vibrations les plus amples**
Ricardo Devesa

Sur quoi devrais-je me concentrer lorsque j'observe une conception architecturale ? Cette question, qui est souvent posée par les critiques lorsque nous nous apprêtons à rédiger un texte parlant d'un bâtiment, vient également à l'esprit des photographes qui se préparent à documenter un projet. Que devrais-je prendre en photo ? Ses façades, ses détails, ses espaces uniques, autrement dit, ses conditions architecturales, comme le font 99 % des photographes de bâtiments ? Force est de constater que très peu de reportages photo et de textes critiques se fixent l'objectif de révéler les relations d'un bâtiment avec son environnement, qui ont tendance à être moins évidentes. En fin de compte, en tant que critique et photographe, nous avons tous les deux choisi de décrire un objet et les relations qu'il établit avec ses environs. L'un à travers des mots, l'autre à travers des images. Et lorsque le travail est réalisé en tandem, les deux lectures s'enrichissent mutuellement. Ce fut en effet notre cas. En octobre 2017, en tant qu'éditeur de ce livre, j'ai rejoint Jordi Bernadó lors de sa séance photo et il m'a accompagné dans la rédaction de ce texte.

Lors d'une rencontre entre architectes, j'avais proposé une approche du bâtiment faisant l'objet de cette monographie—qui est située sur le Lot E8, dans le 17e arrondissement de Paris à Clichy-Batignolles—reposant sur les «bonnes vibrations» qu'il suscite à deux niveaux de rapprochement : la proximité et l'éloignement, c'est-à-dire entre les deux blocs s'élevant au-dessus de leur infrastructure commune, et entre le complexe dans son ensemble et ses environs. Dans chaque cas, notre objectif était de révéler les logiques relationnelles de la conception. Dans le même esprit, nous avons divisé le contenu de ce livre en deux parties intitulées « Zoom arrière » et « Zoom avant ».

À quel point est-ce que ces relations sont étroites ou

divergentes ? Les échos entre les deux blocs sont rendus explicites à travers leur jeu dynamique de volumes dans les renfoncements et les saillies, à travers les références subtiles, les parallélismes et les contrastes entre leurs textures matérielles et les finitions répétitives de leurs enveloppes respectives : métallique, blanche, lisse et perforée dans un bloc, et des lamelles de verre pliées dans l'autre. Quelle est, par ailleurs, l'étendue des relations qu'ils établissent avec leur environnement ? Quels sont les pièces et les éléments à travers lesquels les architectes comptaient faire « vibrer » leurs bâtiments ? Lors de notre visite du bâtiment et de ses environs, nous avons tous les deux découvert quelques-unes de ces relations que Jordi a parfaitement recueillies dans les photos suivantes, et qui ont servi de base à mon analyse. Nous avons séjourné à l'hôtel Inn Paris-Porte Clichy, situé à environ 900 mètres au nord de l'immeuble. La première photo de Jordi fut prise depuis la fenêtre de sa chambre d'hôtel. Au premier plan, on voit un bâtiment haussmannien isolé, faisant face au boulevard Victor Hugo. Derrière le bâtiment, on aperçoit le boulevard périphérique, cette voie rapide circulaire faisant le tour de Paris et de ses 20 *arrondissements*, qui fut construit sur les fortifications ajoutées par Haussmann à la capitale en 1859. En bas à droite, on voit une partie du Tribunal de Grande Instance, un complexe du palais de justice conçu par Renzo Piano Building Workshop en tant que produit phare du projet ambitieux du nouveau district de Clichy-Batignolles. C'est aujourd'hui l'un des plus hauts immeubles de Paris (160 mètres). En effet, le palais de justice a été conçu dans le plan pour devenir un nouveau point de repère en ville, au même rang que La Défense, l'Arc de Triomphe, la Tour Eiffel et le Sacré-Cœur.

En arrière-plan de la photo, on voit les grues de construction travaillant sur le site et, si l'on regarde de plus près, au-dessus de la construction, on voit le sommet du bloc terrassé en verre qui fait l'objet de cette monographie. À l'échelle urbaine, le projet représente l'horizon de ce nouveau district qui concorde avec la dimension encore plus grande du palais de justice.

Au cours de la première journée de notre visite, nous avions parcouru tout le 17e arrondissement. Ce fut un dimanche. Le parc Martin Luther King, un espace urbain au cœur du projet, débordait de monde. Le bâtiment du Lot E8 est situé à côté de la voie ferrée menant à la gare Saint-Lazare. L'infrastructure commune aux deux blocs inclut une petite cour intérieure qui, avec le toit-terrasse, devient une extension du parc. La végétation se glisse entre les bâtiments et, à leur tour, les bâtiments se fondent dans le parc. Rares sont les nouvelles conceptions de la zone ayant proposé ce type de porosité et d'intégration avec le poumon vert du district.

Le lendemain, lundi, nous avions visité le secteur ouest de cette ambitieuse opération de planification urbaine qui, à ce moment-là, était encore en phase de construction. Nous avions grimpé sur le toit d'un des bâtiments achevés. Jordi avait photographié la façade opposée, à l'est, où se trouve le bâtiment E8. Le diptyque de la vue panoramique s'étend du Sacré-Cœur, au sud, jusqu'au nouveau palais de justice, au nord. Sous cet angle, nous constatons à nouveau la stratégie utilisée par les architectes pour relier leur bâtiment au parc. De même, on peut deviner les contiguïtés entre le bloc blanc (adjacent à la voie ferrée) et celui situé deux rues au nord (e-10b, conçu par TOA+AASB). En revanche, les transparences et les reflets dans le bloc en verre entrent en contact avec le bâtiment voisin au sud (e-5, conçu par Francis Soler). Ainsi, lorsque les deux blocs résonnent avec les bâtiments environnants, générant un rythme alternatif, ils sont également perçus comme autonomes les uns par rapport aux autres, provoquant ainsi des vibrations inattendues à l'échelle urbaine.

L'architecture est construite à partir des détails pour définir ses finitions et ses qualités matérielles. Généralement, nos analyses se basent sur un plan rapproché, les unions ou articulations entre les parties matérielles et, ensuite, leurs espaces. Et pourtant, l'éthique d'une conception peut reposer davantage sur ses relations avec l'environnement à plus grande échelle, qui peuvent être dissimulées ou moins visibles. Dans le bâtiment E8, les liaisons avec le parc, la cacophonie des bâtiments voisins et les rapports subtils avec les monuments parisiens sont tous indispensables pour créer de «bonnes vibrations» à tous les niveaux, le transformant ainsi en un site unique.

Ricardo Devesa, architecte et éditeur, urbanNext

ZOOM IN

Page 52_ **Faire vibrer le potentiel des contraintes**

Andrew Ayers

À un moment de l'histoire où le bâtiment culturel—que ce soit musée, philharmonie, opéra—paraît avoir atteint une liberté formelle totale, se permettant toutes les fantaisies, le logement, lui, semble connaître une évolution contraire, se voyant de plus en plus limité par des contraintes préétablies qui étouffent toute possibilité d'innovation. S'il s'agit de construire dans le secteur privé, il y a bien entendu les diktats du marché et les marges de bénéfices que doivent respecter les promoteurs. S'y rajoutent, à notre époque de la transition énergétique, les contraintes liées aux performances thermiques et à la basse consommation, qui impactent fortement les possibilités architecturales. Puis viennent les contraintes réglementaires, qui sont légion : les plans locaux d'urbanisme (PLU), qui déterminent entre autres la hauteur, la volumétrie et l'implantation des constructions ; mais aussi les règlementations en matière d'incendie, qui imposent toutes sortes de limitations. Dans le cas d'une opération en zone d'aménagement concertée, la ville peut imposer des contraintes de programmation et mixité. Et puis arrivent les architectes qui, on l'espère, se contraignent à offrir aux usagers la meilleure des conditions possibles dans le respect de ce dédale de paramètres. Y parvenir relève d'une véritable gageure, la résolution d'un puzzle géant à multiples dimensions.

A Paris, dans le dix-septième arrondissement, c'est exactement à ce type de casse-tête chinois que devait faire face l'équipe formée par l'agence franco-espagnole Gausa + Raveau et l'agence franco-chilienne Avenier-Cornejo (G + R / A-C). L'îlot en question se trouve en bordure d'un parc d'une dizaine d'hectares, conçu par la paysagiste Jacqueline Osty, qui constitue le cœur du nouveau quartier des Batignolles. Le fruit d'une zone d'aménagement concertée lancée en 2005, sur un plan d'urbanisme signé François Grether, l'opération a vu la transformation d'anciens terrains ferroviaires en lieux de vie, avec des exigences énergétiques très ambitieuses : < 50 kWh/m²/an de consommation d'énergie primaire, et 15 kWh/m²/an de consommation de chauffage. L'immeuble en question prévoyait cent-quarante-cinq logements, du T1 au T5, dont quatre-vingt-trois en accession, réalisés pour le compte de la société COGEDIM, ainsi que soixante-deux à loyer maîtrisé, réalisés par Linkcity pour le compte de ICF Habitat, la filiale logement de la SNCF. Mais ce n'est pas tout, car la ville a imposé un programme mixte et social : aux logements se rajoutent un foyer d'accueil médicalisé (FAM) pouvant accueillir quarante personnes lourdement handicapées, ainsi qu'un centre de protection maternelle et infantile (PMI).

Pour G + R / A-C, la situation en bordure d'un équipement aussi exceptionnel que le Parc Martin-Luther-King devait être mise en valeur pour le plus grand nombre. Contrairement aux autres équipes invitées au concours architectural, qui avaient toutes plus ou moins fermé l'îlot, G + R / A-C a ménagé une totale transparence entre le front de parc et l'arrière de l'îlot, laissant un magnifique vide au centre du volume bâti. Suffisamment large pour empêcher les vis-à-vis, cette ouverture assure une luminosité et une aération parfaites à tous les appartements, permettant à la majorité de jouir d'une vue sur le parc tout en laissant la possibilité aux constructions avoisinantes derrière d'en jouir également. Dans le socle de l'immeuble se trouvent le FAM et le centre de PMI ; leurs toitures sont végétalisées pour que la verdure se poursuive jusqu'au fond de l'îlot. Les appartements de COGEDIM et de Linkcity sont répartis sur les deux côtés, les logements en accession sur le front de parc, les unités à loyer maîtrisé à l'arrière. Si l'immeuble varie en hauteur, c'est en fonction des règlements incendie : au-dessus du FAM et du centre PMI, le gabarit est limité, car les textes prévoient un classement en immeuble de grande hauteur (ce qui impliquerait la présence permanente de pompiers sur place) si on place trop d'étages d'habitation sur de tels équipements. Là où le rez-de-chaussée est libre d'équipements, l'immeuble peut s'élever à son aise jusqu'à la hauteur maximale (50 mètres) permise par le PLU. Mais avec un programme aussi dense, comment, après avoir autant évidé le volume bâti, faire rentrer tous les mètres carrés requis ? C'était là le coup de génie : en épaississant les corps de bâtiment au milieu, par le moyen de larges porte-à-faux, la surface requise était atteinte sans nuire aux principes du parti. Cette épaisseur supplémentaire aide, qui plus est, à réduire les déperditions en chaleur, tandis qu'une batterie de panneaux voltaïques sur le toit (déguisé en étage courant) assure l'entier respect des exigences énergétiques.

Grâce aux différentes épaisseurs de ses étages et aux gabarits variables de ses corps de bâtiment, l'ensemble vibre au gré des contraintes de programmation et de règlementations. Mais on peut en dire de même en ce qui concerne les traitements de façade et l'agencement des ouvertures. D'un côté le bâtiment frémit au rythme d'un bardage lumineux en tôle perforée, de l'autre c'est la chatoyante rigueur de vantaux en verre qui cadence les balcons filants. Si les fenêtres sont souvent décalées les unes par rapport aux autres d'étage en étage, ce n'est nullement une recherche esthétique gratuite : les règlementations incendie imposant une distance verticale minimale entre fenêtres, les décaler ainsi permet de les agrandir. Il en résulte une générosité pleinement revendiquée par les architectes, qui se poursuit dans le soin apporté jusqu'aux moindres détails. Une énergie bienveillante vibre dans chaque aspect de ce bâtiment, qui permet de contourner habilement tous les écueils soulevés par les très nombreuses et très diverses contraintes.

Andrew Ayers, journaliste d'architecture, historien.

LE CONCEPT
Page 101_ ZCB Clichy Battignoles LOT E8
Mémoire du Projet

Sauts d'échelle pour comprendre le lieu
Le site est intégré dans le réseau multi-urbain de Paris, de la Grande Couronne et des principaux espaces verts et réseaux infrastructurels. La ZAC Clichy-Batignolles est perçue comme un nouveau paysage de liaison, une grande porte urbaine ouverte le long des grands arcs territoriaux vers la ville historique. Devient une importante plateforme urbaine, un nœud d'échange inséré dans le système de grands espaces relationnels parisiens. Il tiendra un rôle de permutation entre échelles que se soit du point de vue territorial, urbain, environnemental, social, culturel, et infrastructurel. La ZAC agit donc comme un dispositif de résonnance et de transfert multi-urbain.
La ZAC Clichy-Batignolles et le Parc Martin Luther King se fondent en un grand espace relationnel, une interface de lignes de connexion et de relations urbaines : lignes de force, lignes de flux, lignes de liaison et d´interaction.
En résonnance avec les bâtiments voisins, le projet cherche à prioriser le dialogue, la courtoisie et l´élégance urbaines dans une démarche cohérente et sensible qui privilège des mouvements subtils au dessus des gestes imposants.

Un îlot traversant
L'une des caractéristiques fondamentales du projet est la création d'une percée quasi complète dans l'îlot, perpendiculairement au parc Martin Luther King. Cette percée agit comme une véritable extension du parc, le prolongeant au cœur de l'ilot et l'amenant jusqu'à la rue et au delà, jusqu'au lot E9. Ainsi rien ne vient obstruer la vue depuis le parc sur ce dernier et inversement. Le groupe scolaire et les logements jouiront donc également de perspectives relativement dégagées sur le parc. De plus, une grande transparence a été recherchée au niveau du socle du projet, parachevant l'idée d'un lien maximal depuis le parc vers la rue.

Recherche de compacité et de vues
Cette percé constitue également une intégration, très en amont de la conception architecturale, d'une stratégie environnementale. Cette disposition implique en effet de construire des bâtiments plus épais que dans l'hypothèse d'une disposition en U. Les immeubles ainsi créés seront ainsi plus denses et compacts, réduisant considérablement les déperditions énergétiques. De plus, grâce à cette configuration, aucun logement ne sera mono-orienté côté rue. Ils bénéficieront donc tous d'ouvertures sur le parc et d'un ensoleillement optimal.

Des masses en mouvement
Les deux bâtiments constituant les logements sont décomposés en volumes de hauteurs variables, la hauteur du bâtiment le plus haut étant 50m.
Les blocs ainsi créés sont superposés puis décalés les uns par rapport autres. L'objectif est de créer des mouvements dynamiques plus que des volumétries statiques, des rythmes plus que des objets fixes. Ces mouvements et ces rythmes associés à l'architecture déjà riche du contexte immédiat permettent d'inventer une nouvelle "musique de la ville". Ces décalages permettent également de créer plus d'espaces extérieurs et d'optimiser les règles d'urbanisme, notamment les prospects.
La stratégie architecturale de ce projet est le fruit d'une réflexion poussée pour éviter un classement IGH du bâtiment.

Avenier Cornejo
architectes

PARIS
BATIGNOLLES
AMÉNAGEMENT

PBA

Associate Architects:	GAUSA+RAVEAU actarquitectura SLP AVENIER CORNEJO architectes
Project Leaders:	Florence RAVEAU Manuel GAUSA Mickael DOMINGUEZ Vicky LENZ Christelle AVENIER Miguel CORNEJO Olivier SARAMITO Joachim BAKARY
Project Team:	CFERM Ingénierie (utilities) Bureau Michel FORGUE (quantity surveyor) Franck Boutté Consultants (HEQ) Bassinet Turquin (landscaping)
Clients:	LINKCITY ÎLE-DE-FRANCE ALTAREA COGEDIM
Developer:	Paris Batignolles Aménagement
Consultants:	Les produits de l'épicerie (graphic design), EVP engineering (structural frame)
Contractor:	Bouygues Bâtiment Île-de-France
Glass Cladding:	COLT
Exterior Roller Shutters:	GRIESSER
Joinery:	MC France
Flooring:	Compagnie Francaise du Parquet

Good Vibrations
Clichy Batignolles: Lot E8
by Gausa+Raveau actarquitectura,
and Avenier-Cornejo Architectes

Published by
Actar Publishers, New York, Barcelona
www.actar.com

Authors
Manuel Gausa, Florence Raveau (Gausa+Raveau *actarchitecture*), Christelle Avenier, Miguel Cornejo (Avenier-Cornejo Architects)

Edited by
Ricardo Devesa

Graphic Design
Actar Publishers

Translations
Tayssir Azouz
Barbara Finch
Andrew Ayers

Photographic credits:

Jordi Bernadó
Pages: 20, 22, 24, 26, 30 and 38.

Sergio Grazia
Pages: 28, 32, 34, 36, 40, 42, 44, 46, 48, 56, 58, 59, 60, 62, 63, 64, 65, 66, 68, 69, 70, 71, 72, 74, 75, 76, 77, 78, 80, 82, 83, 84, 86, 87, 88, 89, 90, 92, 93, 94, 95, 96 and 97.

Avenier-Cornejo
Page: 91.

Printing and binding
Gráficas Campás, S.A.

Distribution
Actar D, Inc. New York, Barcelona.

New York
440 Park Avenue South, 17th Floor
New York, NY 10016, USA
T +1 2129662207
salesnewyork@actar-d.com

Barcelona
Roca i Batlle 2-4
08023 Barcelona, Spain
T +34 933 282 183
eurosales@actar-d.com

Indexing
English ISBN: 9781945150876
PCN: Library of Congress Control Number: 2017960641

Printed in Barcelona

Publication date: July 2019